Michael Harris • David M[...]

WORLD CLASS

LEVEL 1

STUDENTS' BOOK

Longman

Summary of course content

Learning to learn

A Using World Class
LEARNING TO LEARN

Students' Book

Reading	Skimming the book
Speaking	Book quiz
Learner training	Instructions
Listening	Classroom language

Activity Book

Reading	Skimming the Activity Book
Writing	Activity Book quiz
Learner training	Symbols/Classroom language

B Words
LEARNING TO LEARN

Students' Book

Vocabulary	Classroom objects
Speaking	Guessing game
	Classroom language: asking about meaning
Learner training	Vocabulary books

Activity Book

Learner training	International words
Listening	Sound quiz
Vocabulary	Alphabet game

C People
LEARNING TO LEARN

Students' Book

Listening	Student profiles
Writing	Personal information
Speaking	People game
Pronunciation	Alphabet/Hangman game

Activity Book

Learner training	Learner questionnaire
Punctuation	Names
Listening	Dictation
Vocabulary	Word snake

Module 1: Families

1 The Munsters

Students' Book

Reading	Magazine article
Language focus	**Verb *to be***
Pronunciation	Short forms
Vocabulary	Family relationships

Activity Book

Listening	Identifying family members
Language practice	Verb *to be*
Pronunciation	Short forms
Punctuation	Capital letters
Spelling	Family words

2 Animal families

Students' Book

Listening	Animal quiz
Language focus	**Questions: verb *to be***
Pronunciation	Intonation: questions
Writing	Linking with *and*

Activity Book

Language practice	Questions: *to be*
Language extra	***a/an***

3 A Nepalese family

Students' Book

Reading	A village family
Language focus	***Has/have got***
Pronunciation	Short forms

Activity Book

Listening	Dialogue
Language practice	*Has/have got*
Punctuation	Full stops and capital letters

4 Swiss Family Robinson

Students' Book

Listening	Story
Language focus	**Questions: *Has/have got***

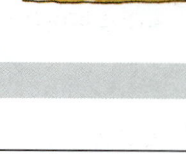

Activity Book

Language practice	Questions: Has/have got
Writing	Survey results
Language extra	**Plurals**

5 Wacky families

Students' Book

Vocabulary	Adjectives
Reading	Descriptions
Language focus	**Possessive adjectives**

Activity Book

Language practice	Possessive adjectives
Pronunciation	Short forms: *'s* (*is* or *has*)
Language extra	**Adjective word order**

6 Fluency

Students' Book

Learner training	Mini-dictionary use/ Instructions game
Reading	Good parents
Speaking	Personal information/Famous person game
Writing	Penfriend letter Project: Imaginary family

Activity Book

Listening/Reading	Cartoon story: *The Silly Family in the Jungle*

7 Language revision

Module 2: Fun

8 Free time

Students' Book

Speaking	Class survey/Guessing game
Listening	Dialogue: national dolls
Language focus	**Present simple: affirmative/ negative**
Pronunciation	Third person singular endings

Activity Book

Language practice	Present simple
Pronunciation	Plural endings

9 Computer games

Students' Book

Speaking	Games survey
Reading	Magazine article: game boys
Language focus	***This/that/these/those***
Writing	Linking: *but*

Activity Book

Language practice	*This/that/these/those*
Language extra	**Irregular plurals**

10 A circus school

Students' Book

Reading	Magazine article: circus school
Language focus	***Can/can't***
Pronunciation	Weak/strong forms

Activity Book

Listening	Dialogue
Language practice	*Can/can't*
Vocabulary	Collocations: *ride/play/watch*

11 Parties

Students' Book

Listening	Dialogue: party questionnaire
Language focus	**Present simple questions**
Pronunciation	Intonation with questions

Activity Book

Listening	Dialogue completion
Language practice	Present simple questions
Language extra	**Question words**
Punctuation	Question marks
Pronunciation	Intonation with questions

Activity Book

Language practice	Present continuous
Punctuation	Name and address
Language extra	**Ordinal numbers**

20 Fluency

Students' Book

Listening	Story: *Boy who cried 'Wolf!'*
Speaking	Guessing game/shopping game
Punctuation	Uses of the apostrophe
Writing	Project: inventing a village

Activity Book

Listening/Reading	Tiddlehampton adventure

21 Language revision

Module 4: The Wild West

22 Native Americans

Students' Book

Vocabulary	Indian life
Reading	The Plains Indians
Language focus	**Regular past simple: affirmative/negative**
Pronunciation	Regular past tense endings

Activity Book

Language practice	Past simple
Spelling	Single/double consonants
Pronunciation	Regular past tense endings

23 A wild west town

Students' Book

Vocabulary	Places
Listening	Tourist information
Writing/Speaking	Directions

Activity Book

Reading	Cowboy life
Language extra	*Why/Because*
Writing	Directions
Vocabulary	Places: old and modern

24 The little house

Students' Book

Vocabulary	Furniture
Reading	Fiction extract
Language focus	**Past simple: verb *to be***
Pronunciation	Weak/strong forms: *was/were*
Speaking	Memory game

Activity Book

Language practice	Past tense: verb *to be*
Punctuation	Commas in lists
Language extra	**Time**

25 Television

Students' Book

Speaking	Television survey
	Expressing opinions
Reading	Television guide
Listening	Dialogue: opinions

Activity Book

Listening	Wild West quiz
Language extra	**Question words: *what/which/who/where/why/when***
Vocabulary	Television programmes
Pronunciation	Short forms

26 Annie Oakley

Students' Book

Listening	Life story of Annie Oakley
Language focus	**Past simple questions**
Speaking	Questionnaire about lives

Activity Book

Language practice	Past tense questions
Reading	Butch Cassidy

Module 6: Planet Earth

36 Galactic tours

Students' Book

Vocabulary	Parts of the body
Listening	Tourist guide
Language focus	**Present simple/continuous**
Speaking	Describe and draw

Activity Book

Language practice	Present simple/continuous
Spelling	Clothes

37 World quiz

Students' Book

Vocabulary	Countries
Reading	Map/notes
Listening/Speaking	Quiz questions
Pronunciation	Word stress
Writing	Country profile

Activity Book

Reading	*A world language*
Pronunciation	Word stress
Language extra	**Farewells**
Punctuation	Commas in numbers

38 Meeting humans

Students' Book

Speaking	Questionnaire
Reading	Guide to humans
Language focus	**Suggestions**

Activity Book

Language practice	Suggestions
Listening	Dialogue
Spelling	Difficult words

39 The living planet

Students' Book

Vocabulary	Weather words
Reading	Travel brochure
Speaking	Memory game
Writing	Notes
Pronunciation	Sounds /æ/ /ɑ:/

Activity Book

Listening	Regions of the world
Language extra	**Article *the* + places**
Punctuation	Capital letters for places
Spelling	*ar* in words
Pronunciation	Sounds: /æ/ /ɑ:/

40 Globetrotters

Students' Book

Speaking	Place survey
Listening	Travel plans
Language focus	***Going to*: plans**

Activity Book

Reading	Plans for school visit
Language practice	*Going to*
Vocabulary	Holiday activities
Language extra	***want to***

41 Fluency

Students' Book

Listening	Science fiction story
Learner training	English in the holidays
Writing	Project: real or imaginary country

Activity Book

Listening/Reading	The Norse Creation Myth

42 Language revision

A Using World Class

A

B

C

D

E

F

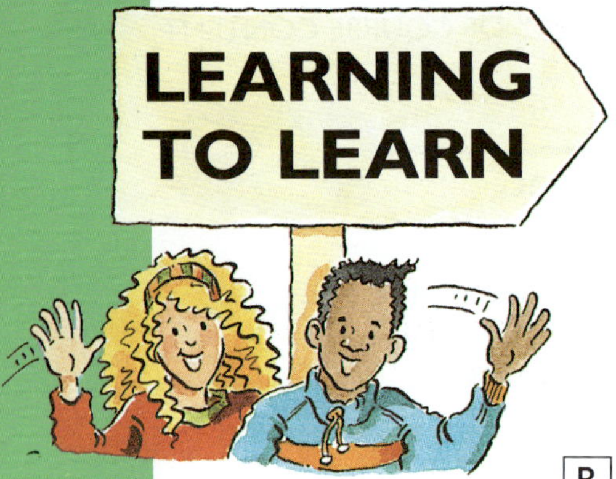

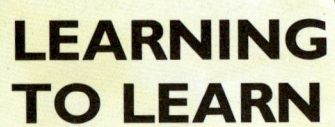

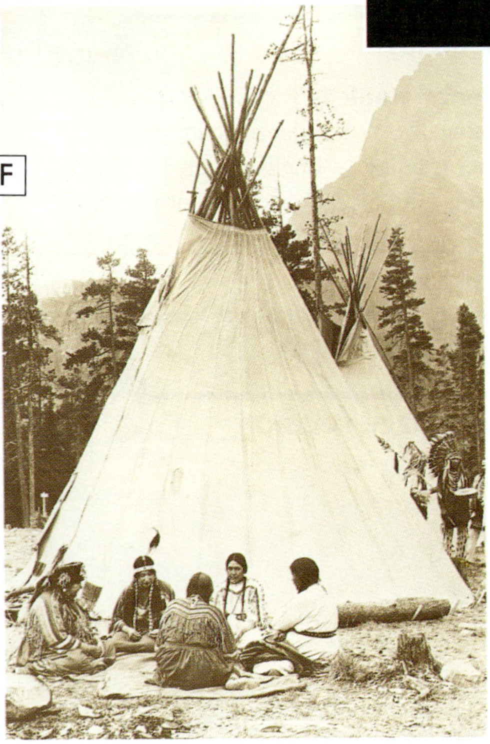

A

These are the titles of the modules in this book. Match them with the pictures.

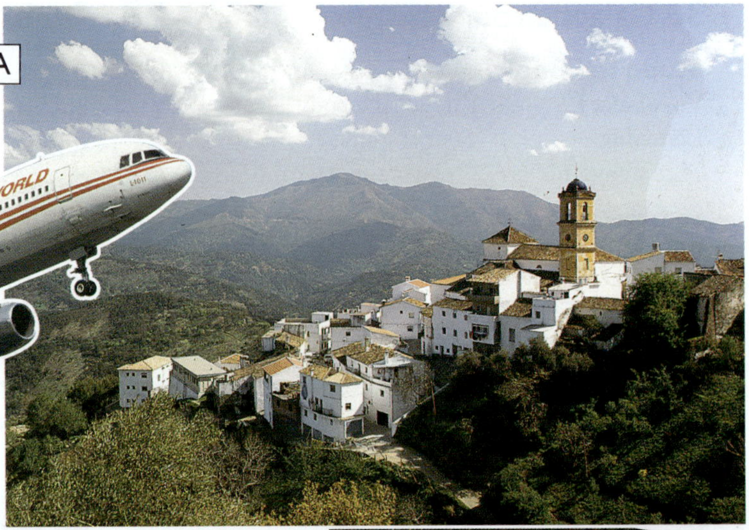

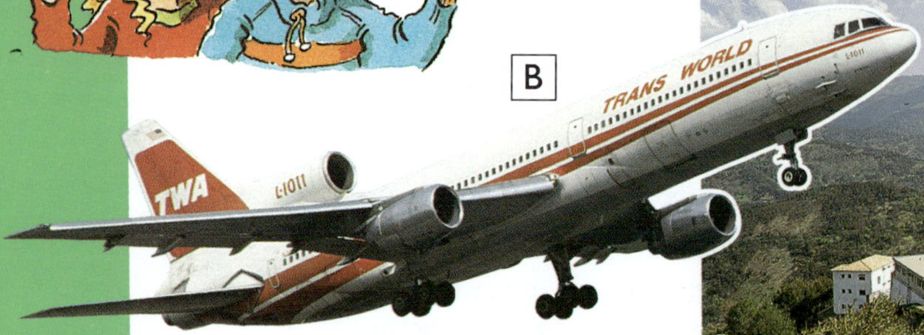

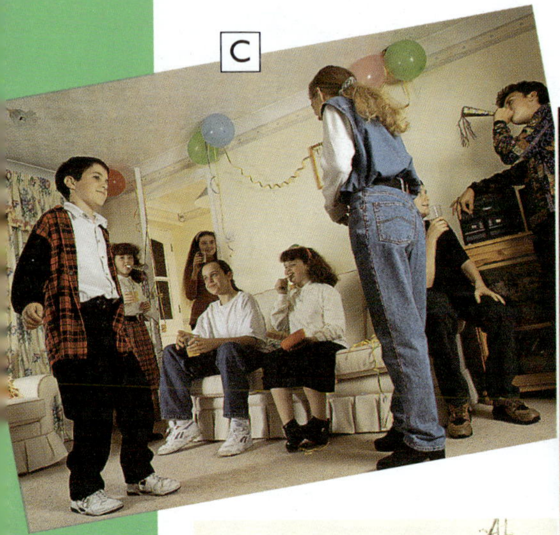

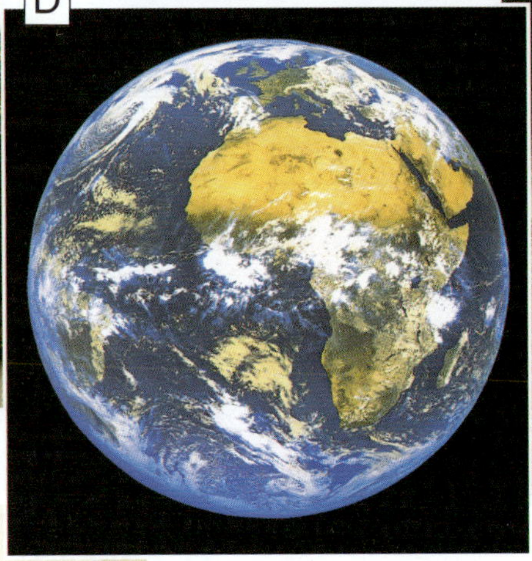

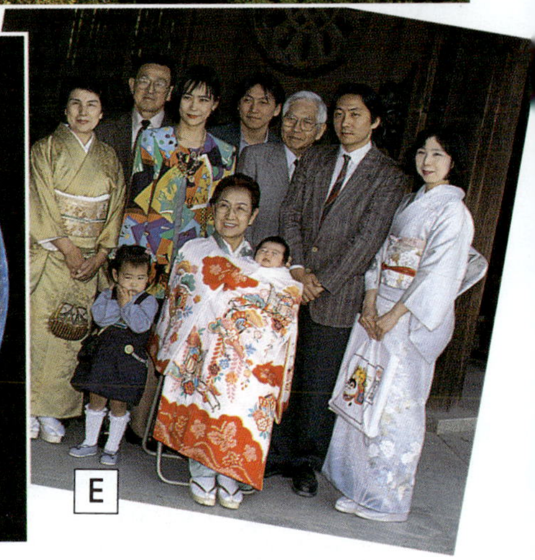

- Families .E. . .
- Fun . . . . .
- Villages . . . . .
- Wild West . . . . .
- Travel . . . . .
- Planet Earth . . . . .

B

Book quiz. Find these in the book.

1 A picture of a party .28. .
2 A photo of The Munsters . . . . .
3 A photo of The Amazon . . . . .
4 Lesson 2: *Animal families* . . . . .
5 Lesson 36: *Galactic tours* . . . . .

C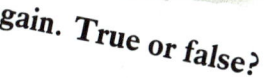

Write a book quiz like exercise B (four pictures or lessons).

1 A picture of a house.
(page 58)

D

In pairs, do your quiz.

A picture of a house.

Here, page 58.

Yes.

E

Listen to the dialogues. Copy and complete the sentences below.

please / understand / please / you

CLASSROOM LANGUAGE

1 I'm sorry, I don't . . . . .
2 Can you speak more slowly, ... ?
3 Can . . . . . repeat that, ... ?

F

Listen and put the instructions below in the order you hear them.

1 . . D . .   3 . . . . .   5 . . . . .
2 . . . . .   4 . . . . .

A

Listen to the story and answer the questions.

B

Read the story again. True or false?

C

Think of an animal. In pairs, ask questions about your partner's animal. Guess what it is.

Language focus
D

Copy and complete the table.

AFFIRMATIVE

I . . . . . from California.

E

Look at the photo and write sentences about the people.

B Words

1
2
3
4
5
6
7
8
9
10
WORLD CLASS
LEVEL 1
LONGMAN New Junior English Dictionary
ROUGH WORK BOOK

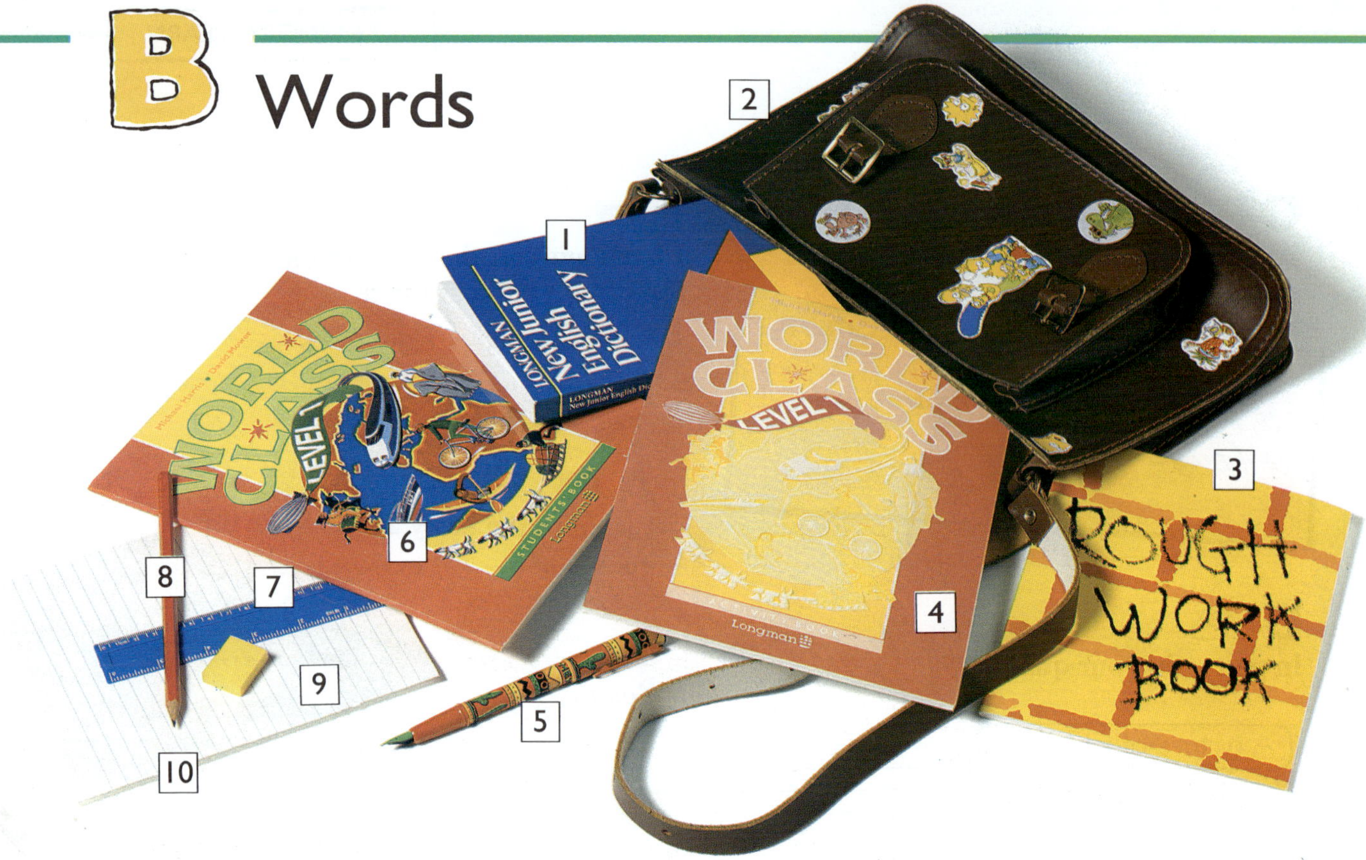

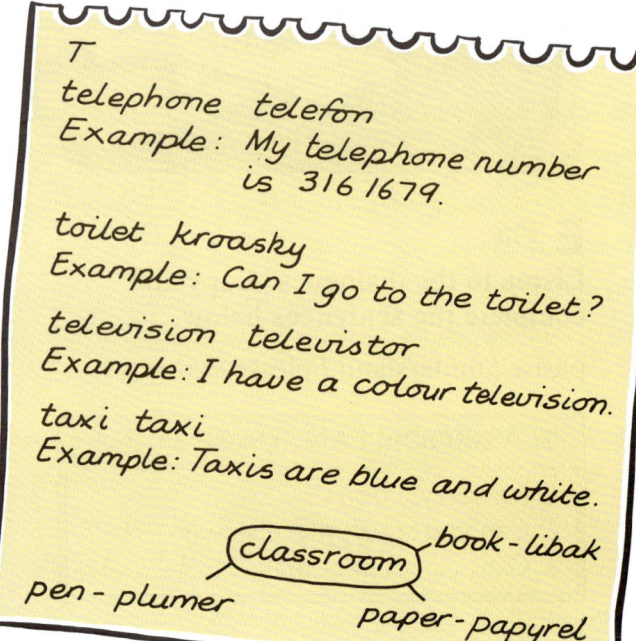

A

Match the words below with the objects in the picture. Use the picture dictionary to help you.

pen . 5 . . .
ruler . . . . .
bag . . . . .
rubber . . . . .
pencil . . . . .
dictionary . . . . .
students' book . . . . .
activity book . . . . .
piece of paper . . . . .
notebook . . . . .

B

In pairs, put some things into your bags. Guess your partner's things.

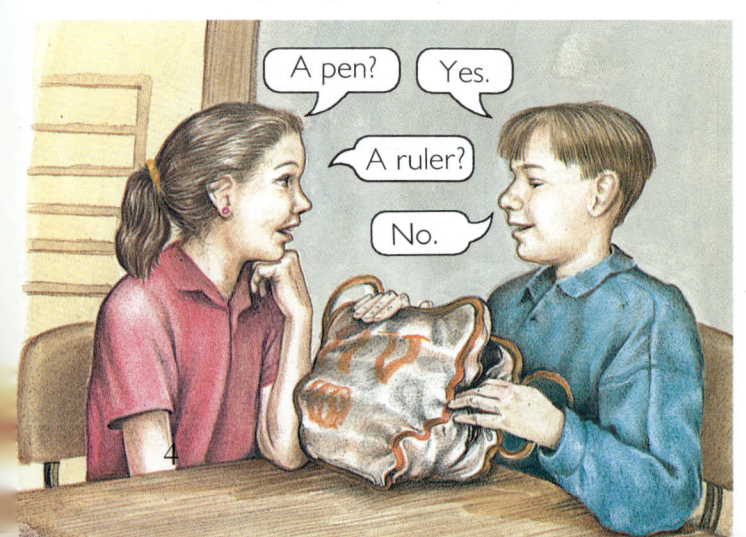

A pen?
Yes.
A ruler?
No.

C

Look at this vocabulary book. Which words are similar in English and the other language?

Example: telephone

What are the words in your language?

T
telephone telefon
Example: My telephone number is 316 1679.
toilet kroasky
Example: Can I go to the toilet?
television televistor
Example: I have a colour television.
taxi taxi
Example: Taxis are blue and white.
classroom
book - libak
pen - plumer
paper - papyrel

D

Write five words in English and five words in your own language on a piece of paper.

apple
Lion

E

In groups, use the example questions below to test the people in your group.

What's <u>diversão</u> in English?

What's <u>village</u> in Portuguese?

Example: A: What's <u>apple</u> in Italian?
B: Pomo.
C: What's <u>león</u> in English?
D: Lion.

F

Listen and repeat the words.

umbrella	cat	green	zebra	house	mother
dictionary	apple	insect	x-ray	jaguar
book	kangaroo	lion	notebook	orange
pen	question	family	ruler	six
taxi	white	yellow	elephant	village

G

Alphabet game.

- In groups, use the alphabet to order the words in exercise F.

apple   book   cat   Er... (out of game)

a b c d e f g h i j k l m n o p q r s t u v w x y z

A B C D E F G H I J K L M N O P Q R S T U V W X Y Z

C People

A 🔊

How old are Georgos and Cristina? Listen and find out.
Listen again and complete the student profiles.

Profile

Name: Georgos Papadopoulos

Home: Greece   Age: ¹ _____

Favourite colour: ² _____

Favourite number: ³ _____

Favourite activity in class: ⁴ _____

Profile

Name: Cristina García

Home: ⁵ _____   Age: ⁶ _____

Favourite colour: blue

Favourite number: ⁷ _____

Favourite activity in class: listening to songs

B 🔊

Listen again. Order the questions.

a) How old are you? . . . . .
b) What is your favourite number? . . . . .
c) Where are you from? . . . . .
d) What is your favourite colour? . . . . .
e) What's your name? . .1. . .

Now listen and repeat the questions.

C ✏️

Look at the the profiles in exercise A. Write your profile.

D 🗨️

Copy the table below. Then ask three students questions and complete the table.

	1	2	3
Name	Georgos		
Age	11		
Favourite colour	red		
Favourite number	3		

E

Play this game.

1 In groups, write one of each of these things on a small piece of paper.
   - a name
   - an age
   - a place
   - a job

2 Put the pieces of paper in four groups (names, places, ages, jobs).

Nancy

Benjamin

87

28

bus driver

India

3 Choose one piece of paper from each group.

4 Ask questions about the other people.

Example: A: What's your name?
B: Nancy.
C: What's your job?
B: I'm a bus driver.
D: Where are you from?
B: I'm from India.
A: How old are you?
B: I'm 87.

5 Tell the class about the people in your group.

   Example: Nancy is a bus driver from India and she's 87!

F

Listen and repeat the letters of the alphabet.

ABCDEFGHIJKLMN
OPQRSTUVWXYZ

G

Play Hangman.

- Guess the letters in the words.
- When you are correct, the teacher writes the letter.
- When you are not correct, the teacher draws a line.
- If the teacher finishes the picture you lose!

Example: 1 E _L E P H A N T_

The Munsters

A

Read the text and match the names with the people in the picture.

Example: 1 = Herman

B

True or false?

1 Grandfather is from Germany.
2 Lily is married.
3 Herman is small.
4 Eddie is nine years old.
5 Marilyn is not a monster.

The Munsters aren't a normal family. They are funny. Grandfather is a vampire. He is from Transylvania and he is 378 years old. His hobby is magic and his favourite drink is blood!

Lily is 140 years old. Her hair is long and black. Her favourite activity is cooking. She is married to Herman.

Herman is from Germany. He is 150 years old. He is very big. One eye is brown and one is green. His favourite television programme is 'The Simpsons'.

Eddie is ten years old. His favourite toy is a doll called 'Woof Woof.'

Marilyn is twenty-three years old. She isn't a monster. Her hair is blonde. Marilyn isn't the daughter. She's Lily's niece.

Language focus: THE VERB 'TO BE'

C

Look at these examples.

> Herman **isn't** (is not) small.
> He**'s** (is) big.
> They**'re** (are) funny.
> They **aren't** (are not) a normal family.

Now complete the tables below.
Note: *isn't* = short form.

AFFIRMATIVE		
I	'm (am)	
You	're (are)	
He / She / (It)	. . . . .	funny.
We / You / They	. . . . .	

NEGATIVE		
I	'm not (am not)	
You	aren't (are not)	
He / She / (It)	. . . . .(. . . . .)	normal.
We / You / They	. . . . .(. . . . .)	

Say the sentences in *your* language.

D

Write sentences using the words below and the verb *to be*.

Example: The Munsters aren't normal.

1 The Munsters / normal
2 The Munsters / funny
3 They / not from England
4 Grandfather / from Transylvania
5 Marilyn / not monster

Pronunciation

E

Listen and write the sentences. Count the words. Short forms count as two words.

Example: We're from California.

Listen again and repeat the sentences.

F

Write information about you on a piece of paper. Use the ideas below.

- Place from   - Age   - Favourite film

Examples: I'm from London.
I'm eleven years old.
My favourite film is *Jurassic Park*.

G

In groups, mix up the pieces of paper from exercise F. One student reads the sentences and the others guess who it is.

H

Look at the family tree below and match the names with the words.

Example: 1 = b)

1 Anna and Paul   a) brother / sister
2 Tom and Mary   b) mother / son
3 Paul and Mary   c) husband / wife
4 Tom and Anna   d) father / daughter

9

2 Animal families

tiger

black panther

lion

A

Look at the pictures. What colours are the animals?

Example: Panther – black

Which animals are from the cat family?

B

Animal quiz. Listen and guess the animals from exercise A.

1 *tiger*   2 . . . . .   3 . . . . .

Language focus:

QUESTIONS: WH-/ YES / NO

C

Look at the word order in these examples.

YES / NO QUESTION	ANSWER
Is it a tiger?	Yes, it is. / No, it isn't.

WH- QUESTION	ANSWER
Where is it from?	Asia.

Listen to the cassette again and match the questions and answers below.

1 **Where** is it from?   a) No, it isn't.
2 **Is it** big?   b) Yes, it is.
3 **What** colour is it?   c) Asia.
4 **Is it** a lion?   d) Yellow and black.

Europe

Africa

South America

penguin

Antarctica

parrot

D

Match the questions and answers.

1 What are your favourite animals?   a) No, they aren't.
2 Are you from America?   b) Black and white.
3 Are they yellow?   c) Prince.
4 Who is your favourite singer?   d) Dogs.
5 Where is it from?   e) No, I'm not.
6 What colour is it?   f) India.
7 Is she from Europe?   g) Yes, she is.

Listen and check your answers.

Pronunciation

E

Listen and repeat the questions from exercise D.
Now ask and answer the questions with your partner.

Example: A: Who is your favourite singer?
      B: Madonna.

F

Think of an animal. In pairs, ask questions about your partner's animal. Guess what it is.

Example: A: Is it a bird? B: Yes, it is.
      A: What colour is it? B: Black and white.
      A: Where is it from? B: Antarctica.
      A: Is it a penguin? B: Yes, it is.

G

Look at the sentences in the boxes.

TWO SENTENCES	ONE SENTENCE
Tigers are black. Tigers are yellow.	Tigers are black **and** yellow.

Now join the sentences below with *and*.

1 Tigers are from India. Tigers are from Siberia.
2 Penguins are black. Penguins are white.
3 Elephants are from Africa. Elephants are from India.
4 Lions are big. Lions are strong.

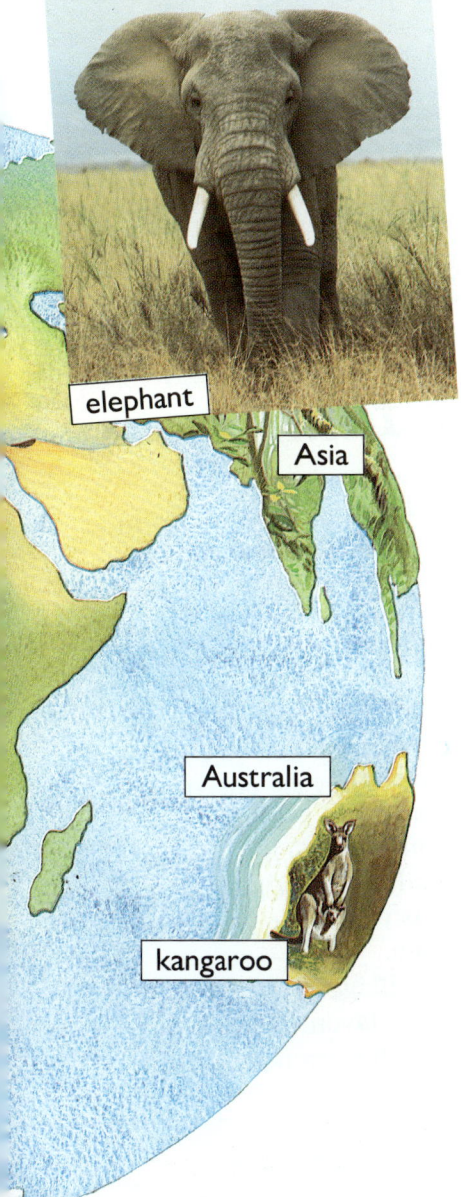

elephant

Asia

Australia

kangaroo

11

3 A Nepalese family

A

Look at the pictures and read the text. Who are the people in the pictures?

1 . . . . .   4 . . . . .
2 . . . . .   5 . . . . .
3 . . . . .   6 . . . . .

B

Read the text again. Copy and complete the table below. Use the picture dictionary to help you.

Things in their house	Animals
3 cupboards	a cat

A village family

1 Jabu and his family are from a mountain village in Nepal. Jabu has got one sister called Pomzi and one brother called Norbu. Pomzi is seven years old and Norbu is a baby. His father, Kepu, is a farmer. Jabu's
5 mother is called Cheuki and his grandmother is called Bajai.

The family isn't rich and they've got a small house in the village. It hasn't got electricity and has only got one window. In the house they've got three
10 cupboards, two small tables and a fire for cooking.

The family has got some animals. They haven't got a dog, but Pomzi has got a small pet cat. Cheuki has got ten hens for eggs. Kepu hasn't got a tractor for his small farm. He's got two oxen.
15 Jabu has lessons with the village teacher and helps his mother and father. His favourite sport is badminton and he plays it with his friends in the village.

Language focus: HAS GOT / HAVE GOT

C
Look at these examples from the text.

> They**'ve got** a small house in the village.
> Kepu has**n't got** a tractor.
> He**'s got** two oxen.
> They **haven't got** a dog.

Copy and complete the tables below. Use these words.

hasn't (has not) / 've (have) / 's (has) / haven't (have not)

AFFIRMATIVE			
I / You	have ('ve)		
He / She /It	. . . . . (. . . . .)	got	a small house.
You / We / They	. . . . . (. . . . .)		

NEGATIVE			
I / You	have not (haven't)		
He / She / It	. . . . . (. . . . .)	got	a dog.
You / We / They	. . . . . (. . . . .)		

Pronunciation

D 📼
Listen to Katy talking about her family. Order the sentences.

a) My dad's got a car. . . . . .
b) I've got a dog. . . . . .
c) We've got a big house. .1. . . .
d) We haven't got hens. . . . . .
e) My sister hasn't got a pet. . . . . .

Listen again and repeat the sentences.

E
Write six sentences about your family, using these words.

a dog / a radio /
an English dictionary /
a telephone / a parrot /
a Prince record /
a cat / a car / a television / a fish

Example: We haven't got a dog. My sister's got a radio.

F
In pairs, guess what your partner and his / her family have got. The first person to guess five things is the winner!

Example: A: You've got a dog.
B: Yes, we have.

G
In groups, play this memory game. If you make a mistake you are out of the game.

I've got a dog called Cecil.

Ana's got a dog called Cecil and I've got a snake called Fred.

Ana's got a dog called Cecil, Marek's got a snake called Fred and I've got a canary called Albert.

 **Swiss Family Robinson**

A

Put the words on the right in the correct list.

Animals	Useful objects
cow	knife

B

Listen to the story and put the pictures (A, B, C) below in order.

1 . . . . .   2 . . . . .   3 . . . . .

C

Listen to the story again. Write the number of these things in the story.

hens / ducks / dogs / plates / forks / books

Example: 10 hens

cow
knife
plate
duck
bottle
book
fork
dog
monkey
pig
matches
tent
hen

Language focus:

QUESTIONS: HAS GOT / HAVE GOT

D

Look at these questions from the story.

What **has Fritz got**?	What **have they got**?
Has he got a monkey?	**Have they got** a cow?
What animals **have we got**?	

Copy and complete the tables below. Look at the word order.

YES / NO QUESTIONS

Have	I / you		
. . . . .	he / she / (it)	got	a monkey?
. . . . .	you / we / they		

SHORT ANSWERS

Yes, I have. / No, I haven't.
Yes, he has. / No, he hasn't.
Yes, they have. / No, they haven't.

WH- QUESTIONS

	have	I / you	
What (animals)	. . . . .	he / she / it	got?
	. . . . .	you / we / they	

E

Use *has* or *have* and the words below to write questions.

Example: Have you got a radio?

1 you / got / a radio?
2 what / she / got?
3 what animals / they / got?
4 he / got / a dog?
5 what / pets / you / got?
6 they / got / a television?

F

Imagine you are on a desert island. Write a list of eight things you have.

Animals: *a dog, two cows and four ducks*

Objects: *matches, a tent, a radio, plates and forks.*

G

In pairs, ask questions about your lists. The first person to guess five things is the winner.

Example: A: Have you got a radio?
   B: Yes, I have. Have you got books?
   A: No, I haven't.

Did you know?

The Swiss Family Robinson called their island 'New Switzerland'.

 # Wacky families

A

Look at the picture of the Silly family and the words and pictures below. Is this information true or false?

Darlene - nose is big

Grandma - hair is blonde

Grandma - short

Rudolf - fat

Horace - hair is long/dark

HAIR dark blonde

long short

EYES brown blue

NOSE big small

TALL SHORT

FAT THIN

B

Look at the picture of the Silly family and read the descriptions. Find one difference in each description.

Example: 1 the picture = five piranha fish
the description = ten piranha fish

1 We're the Silly family. We've got some pets: a tarantula called Maggie, an alligator called Alistair and ten piranha fish. Our house is very silly and it's got a
5 little garden. Our car is very big and has got a TV in it.

My mum is called Gertrude. She's thirty-seven years old. She's very tall and her hair is blonde. Her eyes are green
10 and her nose is small. My dad is called Horace and he's forty years old. He's short and his eyes are blue. His hair is long and dark.

My name's Rudolf Silly and I'm eleven.
15 I am tall and thin. My hair is dark and my eyes are green. My sister Darlene is six. She's very short and fat with blonde hair and blue eyes. Her nose is very big.

My grandpa and grandma are very old.
20 Their house is very small. They haven't got any pets, but they've got lots of books. Grandpa is tall and his hair is short and white. Grandma is short and her hair is black.

Gertrude

Darlene

LIMO 1

Language focus:

POSSESSIVE ADJECTIVES

C

Look at the examples in the box.

> We've got lots of pets. **Our** house is silly.
> She's very tall and **her** hair is blonde.
> He's short and **his** eyes are blue.
> I am tall and thin. **My** hair is dark.
> They've got lots of books. **Their** house is small.

Now copy and complete the table below.

SUBJECT PRONOUNS	POSSESSIVE ADJECTIVES
I	. . . . .
you	your
he	. . . . .
she	. . . . .
it	its
we	. . . . .
you	your
they	. . . . .

D

Complete the text below with these words.

her / his / she / our / my / their / our / we

My name's Gertrude Silly and [1] . . . . .
husband is called Horace. [2] . . . . . have got
two fantastic children. [3] . . . . . names are
Rudolf and Darlene. Rudolf, [4] . . . . . son, is
short and [5] . . . . . eyes are green. Darlene,
[6] . . . . . daughter, is only six. [7] . . . . . is
short and [8] . . . . . eyes are blue.

E

Write three sentences about a person in *your* family, like this:

> My Mum: She is thirty-nine.
> She is tall and thin. Her eyes
> are brown and her hair is dark.

F

In pairs, ask about your partner's person.

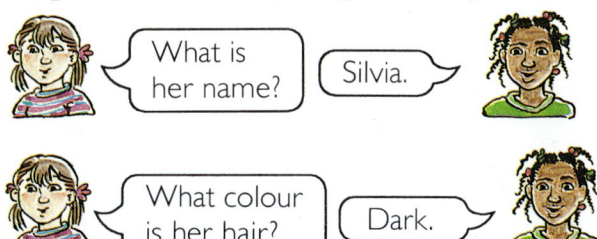

What is her name? — Silvia.

What colour is her hair? — Dark.

G

Guess the person. In groups, one person chooses a person from the Sillys. The others ask questions and guess the person.

Example: A: Is it a man?
B: Yes, it is.
C: Is his hair white?
B: No, it isn't.
A: Is it . . . . . ?

17

6 Fluency

A **Match the words below with the mini-dictionary entries.**

to look after . *5* . . .
hippo . . . . .
parent . . . . .
polar bear . . . . .
babysitter . . . . .

1   a father or mother.

2   a person who looks after children when their parents are out.

3   4

5   to care for. *She* **looks after** *her pet dog.*

B

True or false?

1 Hippos are good babysitters.
2 Baby polar bears like cold water.
3 Elephants are good mothers.
4 The male penguin is a bad father.

Now read the text and check your answers.

Good Parents

Animals are very good parents. Here are lots of examples.

A female hippo is a good baby-sitter! She looks after the babies of other hippos.

Mother elephants look after baby elephants very carefully. The babies walk under them.

Baby polar bears think cold water is horrible! Their mothers teach them to swim. When they are six months old they are excellent swimmers.

The male penguin has got a difficult job! He sits on the egg for two months. He is cold and hungry. When the baby is born, the mother returns and looks after it.

C

In pairs, ask your partner about these things.

- *You*: name / age / hair / eyes
- *Your family*: names of brothers and sisters / names of parents / home
- *Your favourite things*: animals / singer

Example: A: What colour are your eyes?
B: Brown.

D

Guess the person. In groups, one person thinks of a famous person. The others ask questions to find out who it is.

Example: A: Is it a woman?
B: No, it isn't.
C: Where is he from?
B: The USA.
A: Is it Prince?
B: Yes, it is!

E **LEARN TO LEARN**

Instructions game. Read the instructions in the box and do the activities. You have got ten seconds for each activity.

- *Think* of an animal. *Draw* the animal on a piece of paper.
- *Give* the paper to your partner.
- *Guess* your partner's animal and *write* the name on the paper.
  Example: cat
- *Write* two sentences about the animal.
  Example: It is big. It is black.
- *Join* the sentences with *and*.
  Example: It is big **and** black.
- *Say* the sentence. *Repeat* your partner's sentence.

F

Read this letter and write a reply.

Dear...
   Hello! My name's Fatima. I'm twelve. I've got dark hair and brown eyes. My dad is called Ali and my mum Fatima. I've got one brother, Brahim, and one sister, Aisha. What are the names of your family?
   My favourite animals are cats and my favourite colour is blue. My favourite singer is Prince. He's fantastic! What are your favourite things?
From
Fatima

Project

G

1 **Invent a family. Use the table to write notes about the people in the family.**

Name	Clive (brother)	
Age	13	
Description	big green eyes / long hair / small nose	
Favourite things	black / piranhas / Hard Rockers	

2 **Use your notes to draw a picture and write a description of one of your family.**

Clive

His name is Clive and he is thirteen. His eyes are big and green and his hair is long...

19

7 Language revision

Language practice

A

In pairs, make sentences from the words in the picture. You have got five minutes!

Example: **Her hair is brown.**

BROWN

DARK

BIG RED BLONDE

SHORT LONG

HAIR EYE NOSE

IS ARE

THEIR

MY HER HIS

YOUR OUR

Vocabulary

B

Alphabet game. In groups, one person chooses a letter. Each person thinks of words that start with the letter. When you can't say a word you are out.

Example: A: M . . . mother
B: my
C: man
D: er . . . (out of game)

Pronunciation

C 📼

Listen and write the sentences. Then count the words.

$$1\ \ 2\ \ 3\ \ 4\ \ 5\ \ 6$$
Example: He hasn't got a pet. = 6 words

Listen again and repeat the sentences.

D 📼

Alphabet bingo. Copy the card below and write a letter in each square. Then listen to the letters on the cassette. If you hear your letter, cover it. When you have got nine squares, shout *Bingo!*

F	G	A
I	E	Z
C	L	O

E

Spelling quiz. Choose ten words from your vocabulary book. In groups, ask questions.

> **CLASSROOM LANGUAGE**
>
> How do you spell *parrot?*

Example: A: How do you spell *parrot?*
B: P – A – R – O – T.
A: No, wrong.
C: P – A – R – R – O – T.
A: Correct! One point.

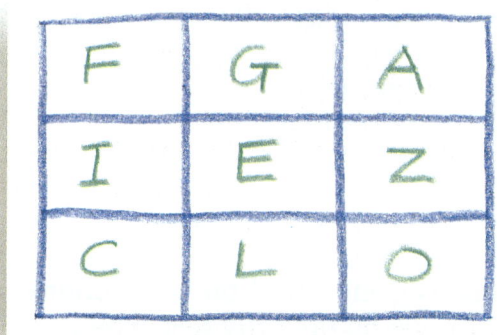

Test yourself

F
Complete Katy's composition with the words below.

got / are / hasn't / are / my / has / her / haven't / is

In our family, animals [1]. *are* . very important. We've got three dogs, two cats, one horse, three rabbits and three fish.

   Daddy [2] . . . . . (not) got a pet. Mummy [3] . . . . . got a brown and white dog called Bouncer. I've got three goldfish. Their names [4]. . . . . Harry, Doris and Kevin. My sister Mary has [5]. . . . . a cat called Patch and a rabbit called Olga de Polga. [6]. . . . . brother Tom is nine and he's got a cat called Tiger and a black rabbit called Herbert. Ana is six and [7]. . . . . rabbit is called Rose. Grandpa has got a very old dog, Daisy.

   We've also got family animals. Basil [8] . . . . . a black and white dog. Markus is a small horse and he is very fat. We've got ten hens. They [9]. . . . . got names!

G
Correct the mistakes in the sentences.

Example: 1 = is

1 My sister *has* ten years old.
2 My *fathers* are called Jean and Marie.
3 Angela is from Buenos Aires. *His* brother is called Ernesto.
4 Have *got you* a pet?
5 She *got* two sisters.
6 Where *you are* from?

H
Do the Module check on page 92.

Do the Module check on page 92.

Language check

THE VERB TO BE

Affirmative
I'm twelve years old. (**I am**)
He / She / It**'s** famous. (**he is**)
You / We / They **'re** from Brazil. (**you are**)

Negative
I'm **not** from New York. (**am not**)
You **aren't** British. (**are not**)
He / She / It **isn't** blonde. (**is not**)

QUESTIONS

Who is your favourite singer?
Where are you from?
What colour is it?
Are you from America?
Is it black?

HAS GOT / HAVE GOT

Affirmative
I / You / We / They **'ve got** two sisters.
She / He / It **'s got** one brother.

Negative
I / You / We / They **haven't got** a dog.
She / He / It **hasn't got** a cat.

Questions
Has he / she / it **got** a car?
Have I / you / we / they **got** a horse?

SUBJECT PRONOUNS AND POSSESSIVE ADJECTIVES

I am from Rome. **My** name is Luigi.
You are Spanish. **Your** name is Carmen.
He is Moroccan. **His** name is Ahmed.
She is French. **Her** name is Françoise.
It is from China. **Its** name is Chu-Lin.
We are from Greece. **Our** names are Nikos and Sophia.
They are from Turkey. **Their** names are Gül and Ali.

book

stamps

national doll

chess

badges

comic

coins

computer games

A

Look at the photo.
List your hobbies.

play table tennis
make models
collect stamps
read books

B

In groups, read your list. What are the favourite hobbies in each group?

Example: coins (4 people)
comics (3 people)

C 📼

Look at the photo of Miriam and the questions below. Guess the correct answers. Listen and check your answers.

1 She collects:
   a) badges. b) national dolls. c) coins.
2 She has got:
   a) fifteen. b) twenty. c) twenty-five.
3 Her favourite doll is:
   a) Japanese. b) Spanish. c) Russian.

tennis

models

table tennis

Language focus: PRESENT SIMPLE

D

Listen to the sentences and fill in the gaps with these words:

go / play / collect / goes / give / understand

> 1 I *collect* national dolls.
> 2 **You** *collect* dolls.
> 3 **She** . . . . . to different countries.
> 4 **We** . . . . . on holiday.
> 5 **They** . . . . . me a doll.
> 6 I don't . . . . . with the dolls.
> 7 **You** don't . . . . . with the dolls.
> 8 **He** doesn't . . . . .
> 9 **We** don't . . . . . him the dolls.
> 10 **They** don't . . . . . dolls.

Now copy and complete the tables.

AFFIRMATIVE		
I / You	. . . . .	
He / She / It	collects	coins.
We / You / They	. . . . .	

NEGATIVE			
I / You	don't		
He / She / It	. . . . .	collect	coins.
We / You / They	. . . . .		

E

Write seven sentences with the present simple.

Example: We don't watch TV.

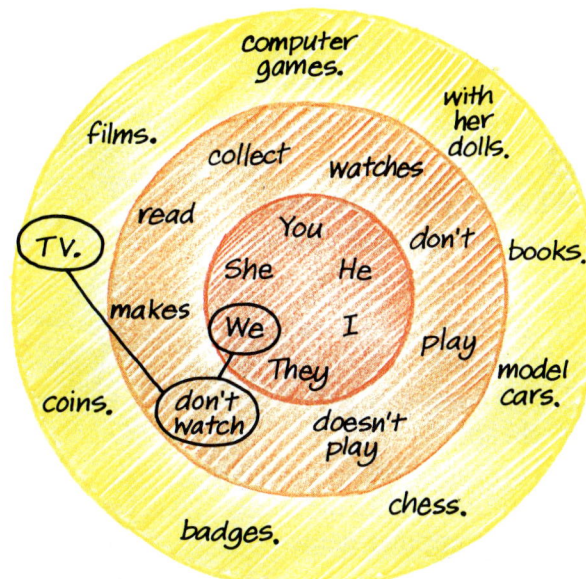

Pronunciation

F

Listen to these words.

Group 1	*Group 2*	*Group 3*
walks	runs	danc*es*

Listen and put the words below in group 1, 2 or 3.

plays / collects / makes / watches / looks / reads

Listen again and repeat the words.

G

In pairs, say true and false sentences about your family's hobbies. Your partner guesses the false sentences.

Example: A: My sister collects dolls.
> B: True.
> A: No, false!

9 Computer games

A

In groups, say what games you like. What are the favourite games in the group?

Example: We like board games and cards.

B

What do you know about computer games? Answer the questions below.

1 Are the Mario Brothers popular?
2 Are computer games cheap?
3 Have they got animals and monsters in them?
4 Are computer games violent?
5 Are they bad for children?

Now read the article and compare your answers.

dominoes

cards

board game

word game

computer game

The Game Boys and Girls

1 At a summer school in England, I ask some students, 'Who is the President of your country?' Half of them know. 'And who are the Mario Brothers?' They *all* know. The
5 Mario Brothers are, of course, characters in a computer game.

Computer games are not cheap, but they are very popular. Ivan has got a new game. 'I like this game. It has got animals and monsters
10 in it.' 'I don't like that one, it's violent. I like those games with blocks,' says Sandra.

Are computer games bad for children? 'No,' says Daniel. 'These games are just good fun!'

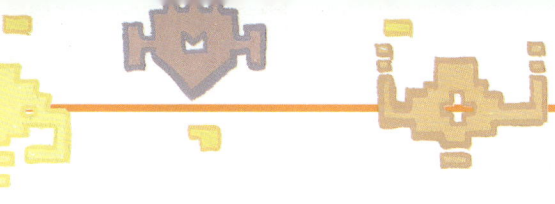

Language focus:

THIS / THAT AND THESE / THOSE

C

Look at these examples.

this game	that game
these games	those games

Now write sentences about the pictures below.

Example: 1 These are dolphins.

dolphins

dragons

dinosaur

blocks

balloon

penguins

D

In pairs, draw five things from this module. Look at your partner's pictures. Ask and answer, like this:

A: What's this?
B: It's a dolphin.
A: What are those?
B: They're tigers.

E

Look at the sentences in the boxes.

TWO SENTENCES

I like computer games with blocks.
I don't like violent games.

ONE SENTENCE

I like computer games with blocks **but** I don't like violent games.

Now join these sentences.

1 Daniel likes games with dragons. He doesn't like games with blocks.
2 Susan likes games with cars. She doesn't like violent games.

Write three sentences with *but* about the games you like.

Joke!

Q: What dog hasn't got a tail?
A: A hot dog!

10 A circus school

A

Classify the activities below. Easy (E) or difficult (D)?

Juggle

Climb a rope

Do Somersaults

Ride a unicycle

Walk on stilts

Walk the tightrope

B

Read about the Circus School. Match the titles with the paragraphs.

- Walking on stilts
- Juggling
- The circus school

1 Students at the Children's Circus in Leeds like school. They make friends and have fun. They can do lots of different things. 'Peter, our teacher, helps us when we can't do things,' says Kristian. 'And we haven't got animals here, which is good.' ▶

◀ **2** Emma and Peter aren't very tall, but when they are on stilts they are enormous! 'Now I can walk on stilts with no problems,' says Emma. 'But I can't run!'

3 Martin Johnstone can ▶ juggle lots of different things – toys, glasses, cheese. 'I want to learn lots of different acts,' says Martin. 'I can't walk the tightrope, but I can juggle and I can ride the unicycle.'

Language focus: CAN / CAN'T

C

Look at these examples.

Martin **can** juggle.	They **can** walk on stilts.
She **can't** juggle.	They **can't** run.
Can he ride the unicycle?	**Can** they juggle?
Yes, he **can**.	No, they **can't**.

Now copy and complete the tables below.

AFFIRMATIVE		
I / You / He / She / It	. . . . .	walk on stilts.
We / You / They		

NEGATIVE		
I / You / He / She / It	. . . . .	walk on stilts.
We / You / They		

QUESTIONS		
. . . . .	I / you / he / she / it	walk on stilts?
	we / you / they	

How do you say *can* and *can't* in your language?

D

Write sentences about what you *can/can't* do.

Example: I can ride a bicycle.
I can't walk on stilts.

1 ride a bicycle
2 walk on stilts
3 ride a horse
4 juggle two oranges
5 ride a unicycle

6 walk the tightrope
7 play tennis
8 play football
9 carry a person
10 do a somersault

Pronunciation

E 📼

Listen and write the sentences. Then count the words.

Example: Can¹ you² ride³ a⁴ bicycle?⁵

Listen and repeat the sentences.

F

In groups, imagine one person is the teacher of a circus school. He/She asks questions to choose one person for the school.

Can you walk on stilts?

No, I can't.

Yes, I can!

Tell the class who you choose.

Example: Maria. She can walk on stilts and she can juggle oranges.

A

Read the questionnaire. Then listen to Mark and Susan doing it. Write down their answers. What is their score?

Example: Mark 1 = b   2 = a

Are you a Party Person?

1 Do you like parties?
a) Yes, they are fantastic.   b) They are OK.   c) No, I don't like them.

2 When you go to a party, who do you talk to?
a) One or two friends.   b) Different people.   c) Nobody.

3 When the music starts, do you dance?
a) Yes, with a friend.   b) No, I sit down.   c) Yes, with different people.

4 When people play party games, what do you do?
a) I go home.   b) I watch the games.   c) I play the games.

What is your score?
1 a = 3   b = 2   c = 1
2 a = 2   b = 3   c = 1
3 a = 2   b = 1   c = 3
4 a = 1   b = 2   c = 3

Total
10 – 12 You love parties. You are a real party person!
7 – 9 You quite like parties.
4 – 6 You don't like parties!

Language focus 1:

PRESENT SIMPLE: YES / NO QUESTIONS

B

Look at these examples.

AFFIRMATIVE	QUESTION
You like parties.	Do you like parties?

How do you say the two sentences in your language?

C

Look at the tables below. Note: He likes parties. Does he like parties?

YES/NO QUESTIONS			
Do	I / you	like	parties?
Does	he / she / (it)		
Do	we / you / they		

SHORT ANSWERS
Yes, I do. / No, I don't.
Yes, she does. / No, she doesn't.
Yes, they do. / No, they don't.

Use *do* or *does* and the words below to write questions.

Example: 1 Do you like parties?

1 you / like / parties?
2 he / play / games?
3 they / talk / to friends?
4 she / dance?

Language focus 2:

WH - QUESTIONS

D

Look at the table below.

WH-QUESTIONS			
What	do	I / you	do?
	does	he / she / (it)	
	do	we / you / they	

Now use *do* or *does* and the words below to make questions.

Example: 1 What music do you like?

1 What music / you / like?
2 Who / she / talk to?
3 What games / he / like?
4 What / they / do?

Pronunciation

E

Copy the questions below. Listen and mark the intonation.

Examples: Do you like parties?

What do you do?

1 Do you go to parties?
2 What music do you like?
3 Who do you talk to?
4 Do you play games?

Listen again and repeat the questions.

F

Use the questionnaire in exercise A to interview your partner. What is his/her score?

12 Magic

Match the instructions (A–E) with the pictures (1–5).
Then listen and check your answers.

1

coin

glass
of water

scarf

2

coin under
the glass

3

take away
the scarf

4

5

B
Hold the glass and
cover it with the
scarf. Don't put the
coin in the glass. Hold
it under the glass.

E
Take away the scarf
and show people the
coin. They think it is
in the water.

D
Take away the scarf.
Now you can't see
the coin!

C
Take a coin, a scarf
and a glass of water.
Now you can do the
trick!

A
Cover the glass with
the scarf again. Hide
the coin in your
hand. Put the glass
and scarf on the
table.

Language focus: IMPERATIVES

B

Complete the tables with these words.

affirmative / negative

> . . . . .
>
> **Cover** the glass with the scarf.
> **Open** your books at page 34.
> **Listen** to the interview.

> . . . . .
>
> **Don't put** the coin in the glass.
> **Don't write** in your books.
> **Don't look** at the picture.

How do you say the verbs in these sentences in your language?

C

Instructions game.

- In groups, write four instructions on different pieces of paper. Use these words.
  Verbs
  put / take / close / open / look at / pick up
  Objects
  piece of paper / pen / book / ruler / activity book / a coin
  Positions
  in your bag / (on) your desk / in your left hand / in your right hand

  Example: **Open** your book!

- Mix up the pieces of paper.
- One student takes a piece of paper and reads the instruction.
- The last person to follow the instructions is out of the game!

D

Look at this trick.

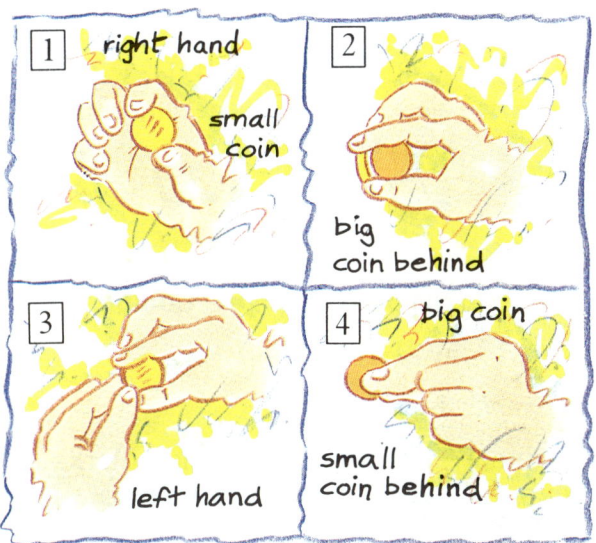

Now complete the instructions with these words.

hold / put / hold / put / show / don't show

Example: 1 = hold

. . ¹ . . a small coin in your right hand.
. . ² . . a big coin behind it: ◖▬◗
. . ³ . . the people the small coin,
. . ⁴ . . them the big coin.
. . ⁵ . . the coins in your left hand.
. . ⁶ . . the small coin behind the big coin.

Now the people can see the big coin, but they can't see the small coin!

E

In pairs, do the trick in exercise D.

> ## Joke!
>
> Q: What is blue, red, green and yellow and can speak English?
> A: A parrot!

13 Fluency

A

Listen to the song. Which of these things can you hear?

Numbers: 1, 2, 3, 4, 5, 6, 7, 8, 9, 10, 11, 12
Letters: A, B, C, D, E, F, G, H, I, J, K, L, M
Colours: black, white, green, red, pink, brown, yellow, grey, orange, blue

B

Listen to the party dialogue. Complete it with these words.

you / I / my / I / you / I

Example: 1 = My

MARK: Hello. [1] . . . . . name's Mark.
VIRGINIA: Hello, [2] . . . . .'m Virginia.
MARK: Where are [3] . . . . . from?
VIRGINIA: [4] . . . . .'m from America.
MARK: Yeah! [5] . . . . . live here. Do [6] . . . . . want a drink?
VIRGINIA: Yes, please. An orange juice please.

C

In groups, imagine you are at a party. Speak to two people. Ask these questions.

- Where are you from?
- What hobbies have you got?
- What things do you like?

Joke!

Q: What has got legs but can't walk?

A: A table!

D

Fun survey. In groups, ask other students these questions.

FUN SURVEY

1 Do you collect anything? . . . .
   (If yes, what do you collect?) . . . .

2 Do you make anything? . . . .
   (If yes, what do you make?) . . . .

3 Do you play sport? . . . .
   (If yes, what is your favourite?) . . . .

4 Do you play computer games? . . . .
   (If yes, what is your favourite?) . . . .

Put the information on a graph and list the favourites.

E LEARN TO LEARN

Answer these questions. Are you a good student?

1 Do you speak English in class?

2 Do you listen to the teacher?

3 Do you use the mini-dictionary when you don't know a word?

4 Do you write important new words in your vocabulary book?

5 Do you come to class with your Students' book, Activity book, vocabulary book and dictionary?

	Yes	No

F LEARN TO LEARN

Put the words in order and make sentences.

go to Can the toilet I please?

use pen please? your Can I

we dictionaries please? Can use

In pairs, ask to use these things.

pen / pencil / ruler / rubber

G

In pairs, plan a party. Write notes about these things.

- when?
- where?
- food?
- drink?
- music?
- games?

Use your notes to make a poster for your party.

 Language revision

A
Board game.

- You need dice and counters.
  Start on this square. does
- When you land on a square,
  write the word on a piece of paper.
- When you have ten words, stop.
- Make different sentences from the
  words you have got. You can use one
  word for different sentences. You get
  one point for every sentence.

Vocabulary

B [LEARN TO LEARN]

**Look at the lessons in this module. Choose
ten new words that are important for you.
In pairs, test your partner with your words.**

Example: What does *chess* mean? How do
you spell *coins*?

Pronunciation

C [LEARN TO LEARN]

**Look at the words in your vocabulary
book. Choose five words that are difficult
to pronounce. Ask your teacher to check
your pronunciation.**

CLASSROOM LANGUAGE
How do you pronounce this, please?

D 🔊

Listen to these two sentences.

a) I like th**is** game.
b) I like th**ese** game**s**.

**Listen and write the five sentences you
hear. *This* or *these*?**

Example: 1 = I like *this* badge.

Listen again and repeat the sentences.

Test yourself

E

Complete Tom's composition with these words.

likes / don't / collects / like / doesn't / can

I've got different hobbies. I ^{1} . *like* . . sport. I ^{2} . . . . . swim and play tennis. I ^{3} . . . . . collect things, but I make model aeroplanes and cars. My sister Anna ^{4} . . . . . like sport. She ^{5} . . . . . things: dolls, badges and stamps. And she ^{6} . . . . . magic. She can do fantastic tricks!

F

Write questions for these answers about the composition in exercise E.

Example: 1 = Does Tom collect things?

1 No, he doesn't.
2 Dolls, badges and stamps.
3 Model aeroplanes and cars.
4 No, she doesn't.
5 Yes, he can.
6 Yes, she can.

G

Correct the mistakes.

1 My sister collect dolls.
2 Can you to play football?
3 What hobbies she like?
4 I don't like these game.
5 Does he collects coins?
6 Don't to close the door.

H

Do the Module check on page 92.

Do the Module check on page 92.

Language check

PRESENT SIMPLE

Affirmative
He / She **plays** tennis.
I / You / We / They **play** chess.

Negative
He / She **doesn't** play tennis.
I / You / We / They **don't** play chess.

Questions
Do I / you / we / they **collect** coins?
Does he / she **collect** coins?
What do I / you / we / they **collect**?
What does he / she **collect**?

THIS / THAT / THESE / THOSE

Singular
I like **this** game. I like **that** game.
What's **this**? What's **that**?

Plural
I like **these** games. I like **those** games.
What are **these**? What are **those**?

CAN / CAN'T

I (you, etc.) **can** ride the unicycle.
I (you, etc.) **can't** walk the tightrope.
Can I (you, etc.) play football?
Yes, I (you, etc.) **can**.
No, I (you, etc) **can't**.

IMPERATIVES

Cover the glass with the scarf.
Don't show people the coin.

 **15** My village

A

Which of these places are near *your* home? Use the mini-dictionary to help you.

factory / mosque / school / bank / shop / restaurant / cinema / park / church / disco / doctor's surgery

B

Read the text below. Which places from the list in exercise A are in Talarrubias?

Example: a church

English competition   José Luis García
                                          6C

My village

I live in Talarrubias with my parents and my brother. Talarrubias is in Spain. It is a fantastic place!

There are old buildings in our village – the houses, the olive-oil factory and my school. There is a beautiful church called Santa Catalina. There are also the usual things in the village – a park, shops, banks, doctors' surgeries, restaurants and there's a disco! There isn't a cinema, but we watch films on video.

Talarrubias is great in August, when we have our local 'fiesta' or festival. I love Talarrubias, but one thing, there isn't a good football team. Maybe one day!

Language focus:

THERE IS / THERE ARE

C

Match these words to make three sentences about Talarrubias.

1 There is	a) old buildings in the village.
2 There isn't	b) a disco.
3 There are	c) a cinema.

Look at the sentences in the boxes below. How do you say the sentences in your language?

SINGULAR

There is a park.

PLURAL

There are four restaurants.

Pronunciation

D

Listen and write the sentences. Then count the words.

Example: 1 There's¹ a² disco³ in⁴ the⁵ village⁶.⁷
= 7 words

Listen again and repeat the sentences.

E

Write six sentences about places near your home.

Example: There is a mosque. There are three shops.

F

In pairs, find out about places near your partner's home.

Example: A: Is there a cinema?
B: No, there isn't.
A: Is there a shop?
B: Yes, there are two shops.

G

In groups, play this memory game.

In the village there's a park.

In the village there's a park and there's a bank.

In the village there's a park, there's a bank and there are two restaurants.

If you make a mistake you are out of the game.

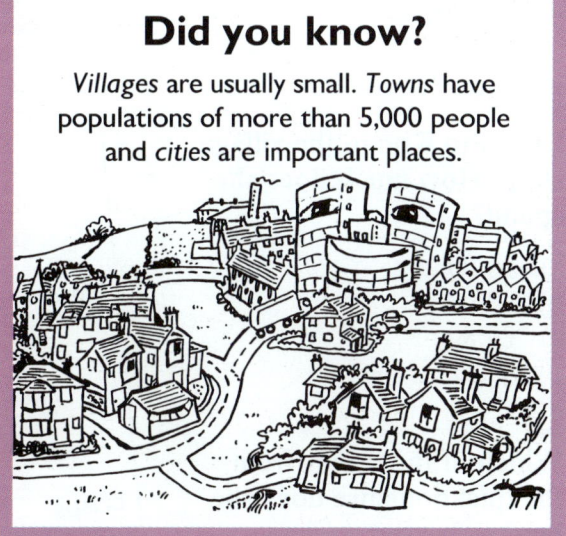

Did you know?

Villages are usually small. *Towns* have populations of more than 5,000 people and *cities* are important places.

16 Village shops

A

In pairs, use the questionnaire on the right to find out what your partner buys.

B

Listen to Kim in the village shop. How much does she spend?

a) £6.00
b) £8.00
c) £9.80

C

Which of the things from the questionnaire does she buy?

What do you buy?

☑ Yes ☒ No

computer games ☐

cassettes ☐

comics ☐

ice-cream ☐

sweets ☐

fizzy drinks ☐

crisps ☐

cakes ☐

clothes ☐

Language focus: SOME / ANY

D

Look at these examples from the dialogue.

> **AFFIRMATIVE**
>
> I've got **some** crisps.

> **NEGATIVE**
>
> I haven't got **any** computer games.

> **QUESTIONS**
>
> Have you got **any** cassettes?

Complete these rules with *some* or *any*.

a) For affirmative sentences we use . . . . .
b) For questions we usually use . . . . .
c) For negative sentences we use . . . . .

E

Complete the sentences with *some* or *any*.

1 I haven't got . . . . . crisps.
2 I've got . . . . . computer games.
3 She hasn't got . . . . . cassettes.
4 Have they got . . . . . comics?
5 They've got . . . . . cakes.
6 We haven't got . . . . . ice-cream.

> ### Did you know?
>
> Villages in Britain often have one 'village shop', where you can buy lots of different things.

F

Complete the shop dialogue with *some* or *any*. Then listen and check your answers.

A: Good morning. Can I help you?
B: Yes, have you got [1] . . . . . comics?
A: No, I'm sorry we haven't got [2] . . . . .
B: Well, I'd like [3] . . . . . sweets. Two of those packets, please. And have you got [4] . . . . . fizzy drinks?
A: Yes, we've got [5] . . . . . cola and [6] . . . . . lemonade.
B: I'd like a can of cola, please. How much is that, please?
A: The sweets are two pounds and the cola is one pound. That's three pounds, please.
B: Three pounds. Here you are.
A: Thank you very much. Goodbye.
B: Goodbye.

Listen and repeat the dialogue.

G

In pairs, practise a shop dialogue like the one in exercise F. Use this price guide to help you.

☐ packet of crisps	£ 0.80
☐ can of cola/lemonade	£ 1.00
☐ packet of sweets	£ 1.00
☐ comic	£ 1.50
☐ cassette	£ 8.00
☐ computer game	£35.00

17 Village people

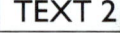

TEXT 1

1 My name is Louise
Midwood and I live near
Wigmore, a small village
in England. In the
5 morning Mum takes me
to school with my brother Anthony.
I don't like school and the school
lunches are terrible. Then, after
school, I play hockey. I love it and
10 I am in the school hockey team. I
want to play in the Olympics,
maybe in 2004! In the evening I
do my homework and watch
television with Anthony. In the
15 summer, Dad sometimes takes us
to the swimming pool, or we
swim in the river near the house.
Sometimes I help Dad with his
bees. He's got thousands of
20 them, and the honey is fantastic.

TEXT 2

1 Julio Barrantes lives in a village near
Cordoba in Argentina. In the morning,
his dad takes him to school with his
sister Elena. He goes to an international
5 school and lessons are in Spanish and
English. He likes them, especially the
computer lessons.
  In the afternoons Julio finishes school
at three o'clock. First, he plays rugby or
10 has rugby practice. He loves rugby and
wants to play for Argentina one day.
Then he goes home by bus. Sometimes he
goes to the swimming pool with Elena or
plays computer games with her. He
15 has got a computer in his room and he
can make new games with it. Next, he
eats with his family. Finally, he does his
homework!

Language focus:
SUBJECT AND OBJECT PRONOUNS

A
Where do you think the two people in the photos are from? Read the texts and find out.

B
Read the texts again and answer these questions.

1 What are their names?
2 Do they like school?
3 What are their favourite sports or hobbies?
4 What other activities do they do after school?

C
Who or what do the underlined words refer to in the texts?

1 My mum takes <u>me</u> to school. (Text 1, line 5)
2 I love <u>it</u> and I am in the school hockey team. (Text 1, line 9)
3 Dad sometimes takes <u>us</u> to the swimming pool. (Text 1, line 15)
4 He's got thousands of <u>them</u>. (Text 1, line 20)
5 His dad takes <u>him</u> to school. (Text 2, line 3)
6 . . . . . or plays computer games with <u>her</u>. (Text 2, line 14)

D

Copy the tables below. Then complete them with the underlined words from exercise C.

SINGULAR	
Subject pronouns	Object pronouns
I	. . . . .
you	you
she	. . . . .
he	. . . . .
it	. . . . .

PLURAL	
Subject pronouns	Object pronouns
we	. . . . .
you	you
they	. . . . .

E

In pairs, complete the sentences with these words.

1 Julio plays rugby after school. He loves . . . . .
2 Louise doesn't like Mrs Green. She hates . . . . .
3 Elena and I go to the cinema. My mum takes . . . . .
4 That is Julio. Look at . . . . .
5 Lessons are boring. I don't like . . . . .
6 Can you speak more slowly? I can't understand . . . . .
7 Mum, please can you take . . . . . to school?

F

Read the text about Julio again and order these sentences.

a) *Finally* he does his homework.
b) *Then* he goes home by bus.
c) *Next* he eats with his family.
d) *First* he plays rugby or has rugby practice.

G

Write about your typical day.

1 Write notes about what you do in the morning / in the afternoon / in the evening.

2 Use your notes to write a short description. Use these words:

first / next / then / finally

H

In groups, find out what people do after school.

What do you do after school?

 I play football.

What do you do next?

 Then I do my homework.

List the activities and draw a graph.

Did you know?

When they leave school, a lot of people from villages go to live in cities.

8 Tiddlehampton

A

Read the descriptions below. Then look at the picture and find the cars and houses for each family.

Example: Boggis family
house = number 5
cars = yellow sports car (8)
small white car (1)

B

Read the descriptions again. List the jobs.

Example: doctor, ...

Sam Boggis

Hi! Welcome to the fantastic village of Tiddlehampton. My mum's the village doctor and my dad's a waiter in the Slugg Arms Hotel.
Can you see that big white house with a big garden, near the church? That's ours. And we've got two cars! My mum's car is that yellow sports car and my dad's car is white and it's very small.

Daphne Stott

Hello, I'm Daphne, Daphne Stott. I'm the teacher at Tiddlehampton school and my husband Eric is a dentist.
Can you see my car? That small yellow car is mine. Where do we live? Well, we love colours and our house is blue, with a red door and pink windows. Pink's my favourite colour, you know! And my daughter Lavinia, she's got a house in the village. That green house, with the blue door and yellow windows, is hers!

Captain Darnley-Smith

Good morning. My name's Darnley-Smith, Captain Darnley-Smith. I'm a businessman and my wife is a policewoman.
Can you see our cars? Mine is very big and it's red. My wife's car is new and it's green. And Rupert, he's my son, he loves cars. That old blue car is his and the big black car is his wife's. Our family has two houses in the village. We live in one and Rupert and Celia live in the other. The green house with big, red garage doors is ours and the small white house near the river is theirs.

42

Language focus 1: POSSESSIVE PRONOUNS

C

Look at these examples from the text.

> That's **ours.**   That small yellow car is **mine.**
> That green house is **hers.**   That old blue car is **his.**
> The small white house near the river is **theirs.**

Now copy and complete the tables below.

SINGULAR	
Possessive adjectives	Possessive pronouns
my	. . . . .
your	yours
her	. . . . .
his	. . . . .

PLURAL	
Possessive adjectives	Possessive pronouns
our	. . . . .
your	yours
their	. . . . .

D ✍

Work in groups. Put fifteen personal objects on the desk. Ask and answer about the objects.

A: **Whose** is this?
B: It's yours.
A: No, it isn't. It's his.

Language focus 2:
POSSESSIVE 'S

E

Match the sentences a) – c) to 1–3 below.

a) My **mum's** car is that yellow sports car.
b) My **dad's** car is white and it's very small.
c) My **wife's** car is new and it's green.

1 My wife has got a new car.
2 My mum has got a yellow sports car.
3 My dad has got a small, white car.

How do you say sentences a), b) and c) in your language?

F ✍

In pairs, cover the text and test your partner about the picture of Tiddlehampton.

Example: A: Whose is this car?
   B: It's Daphne Stott's.
   A: No, it's Mrs Darnley-Smith's.

43

19 Festivals

A

Look at the activities on the right. Which of them can you see in the picture?

Example: buying

B

Listen to the radio programme and answer these questions.

1 Where is the snake festival?
2 What is in the basket?
3 What do the people throw at the statue?

C

Listen again. What other verbs from exercise A can you hear that are not in the picture?

Example: throwing

throwing dancing walking standing

buying selling holding carrying

looking at playing music singing opening taking out

Language focus:

PRESENT CONTINUOUS

D 📼

Listen and complete the sentences with *is* or *are*.

> We **are** looking at the people.
> He ..... carrying a basket.
> He ..... not selling vegetables and the people ..... not buying things.
> What ..... he doing?
> Why ..... they doing this?

Now copy and complete these tables.

AFFIRMATIVE		
I	am (I'm)	
You	are (You're)	walking.
He / She / (It)	..... (.....)	
We / You / They	..... (.....)	

NEGATIVE			
I	am (I'm)		
You	are (You're)	not	singing.
He / She / (It)	..... (.....)		
We / You / They	..... (.....)		

QUESTION			
What	am	I	doing?
	are	you	
	.....	he / she / (it)	
	.....	we / you / they	

E

Put the verbs in brackets into the present continuous.

> Dear Sam
> I am in Cocullo. I (watch) [1] ..... the festival from my hotel window. The musicians (play) [2] ..... but the people (not dance) [3] ..... They (throw) [4] ..... snakes at a statue. A boy (run) [5] ..... and he (carry) [6] ..... a snake! What (you do) [7] ..... now? Is it cold in England?
>
> Anne

F 🗣

In pairs, ask and answer questions about the people in the picture.

Example: A: What is that boy doing?
  B: He is looking at the snakes.

G 🗣

Test your memory. In pairs, close your books. Can you remember what the people in the picture are doing? Write sentences.

Example: A boy is looking at the snakes.

H

In groups, each student mimes an activity. The others guess what he/she is doing. Use these verbs:

eat / drink / study / write / read / play (games / sport / musical instrument) / buy / watch / swim

45

20 Fluency

A

Listen to the story and put the pictures above in order.

B

Listen again. True or false?

1 The first time the boy shouts there is no wolf.
2 The villagers think the boy's joke is very funny.
3 Finally the wolf kills the sheep.

C

In groups, one person thinks of an activity that he/she does (go to school, study English, play football). The others ask questions to find out the activity, like this:

A: Do you *Boggis* at school?
B: No, I don't.
C: Do you *Boggis* at home?
B: Yes, I do.
A: Do you watch television?
B: Yes.

D

Shopping game.

- Work in two groups, group A and group B.
- Group A: make a list of six objects with the price to **sell**.

Example: To sell: *Top Ten* computer game

- Group B: make a list of six objects you want to **buy**.

Example: To buy: *Grand Prix* computer game, packet of crisps

- In groups, buy and sell objects.

Example: Student A: Good morning.
Student B: Hello. Have you got a packet of crisps, please?

- You get one point for every object that you buy or sell.

E

Look at these two different uses of 's.

He's (He is) watching the sheep.
He looks after his father's sheep. (His father has got sheep.)

Put the correct punctuation in these sentences.

1 shes got a brother called john   johns favourite sport is football
2 susans playing a computer game   susans favourite game is top ten
3 richards dad doesnt like television   his dads a dentist

Project option

F

In groups, invent a village.

1 Draw a map of the village with places and buildings. (Look at the example below and the village in Lesson 18.)

2 Choose three people who live there. Write about them, like this:

> This is Maria. She lives in the red house near the river. Her mum works in the village shop and her dad's a taxi-driver. Maria doesn't like school, but she likes English lessons. After school she plays tennis with her sister...

3 Write about the village festival.

4 Check your writing for mistakes.

5 Copy your work and display it as a poster.

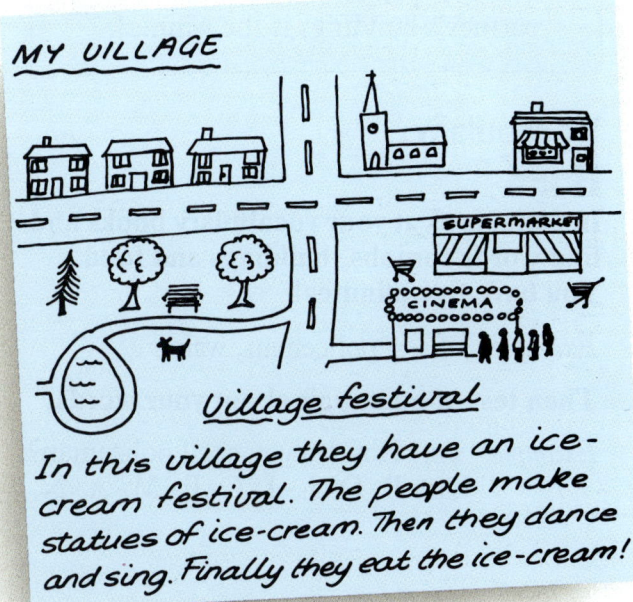

MY VILLAGE

SUPERMARKET

CINEMA

Village festival

In this village they have an ice-cream festival. The people make statues of ice-cream. Then they dance and sing. Finally they eat the ice-cream!

21 Language revision

Language practice

A 🗣
Village game.

- Draw two copies of the grid below. On one copy draw five buildings in different squares.

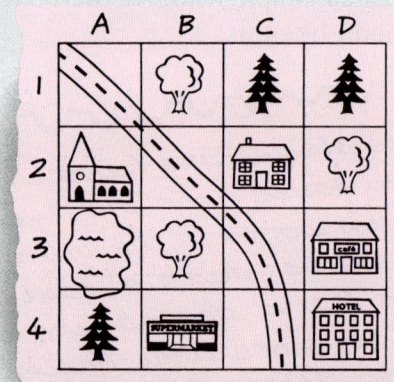

- In pairs, find out where your partner's buildings are. Draw the buildings on the second grid.

  Example: A: Is there a building on C2?

  B: Yes, there's a house.

- The first person to find all their partner's buildings is the winner!

Vocabulary

B 🔲LEARN TO LEARN
In pairs, look at your vocabulary books and find words for jobs, buildings and food. You have five minutes!

Example: jobs = policeman, waiter

Then test another pair about your words.

Example: A/B: How do you spell policeman?

C/D: P - O - L - I - C - E - M - A - N.

Pronunciation

C 🔲LEARN TO LEARN 📼
Look at the stress on this word:

▢ ▫
doctor

Now listen and mark the stress on these words:

1 policeman   3 dentist
2 hotel   4 river

Look at five new words from this module in your vocabulary book. Mark the stress.

D 📼
Listen and repeat the sounds in these three names.

Group 1	*Group 2*	*Group 3*
Tess	Steve	Jane

Copy and complete the table. Use the words below and match them to the three names by sound.

waitress / **de**ntist / **tea**cher
tennis / co**mpu**ter games / **rea**ding
green / **grey** / **red**
ice-cream / **ve**getables / **cakes**
elephant / **sheep** / **snake**

	Tess	Steve	Jane
Job	*dentist*		
Hobby	*tennis*		
Colour of car			
Favourite food			
Favourite animal			

Listen to the descriptions and check your answers.

Test yourself

E
Complete the description with the words.

there is / any / there are / there isn't / some / there are

Eva lives in a village on the island of Crete in Greece. ¹. . . . . three or four shops and ². . . . . a small supermarket, but the village is small and ³. . . . . a cinema or a disco. Eva sometimes goes to Heraklion on Saturday with her mother. ⁴. . . . . some good shops near the main square. Eva doesn't buy ⁵. . . . . clothes, but she buys ⁶. . . . . cassettes and books.

F
Complete the description with the words.

ours / me / him / it / uncle's / dad's

'I go to school in Heraklion and I really like ¹. . . . . Dad takes ². . . . . there in the morning. He's got a restaurant in the village and we sometimes help ³. . . . . Do you want to see the village? That restaurant is my ⁴. . . . . Look at that white house. It's ⁵. . . . .! Can you see the supermarket? That's my ⁶. . . . .'

G
Use the present continuous to make sentences from these words.

Example: What is her mother doing?

1 what / mother / do?
2 Eva / do / English homework
3 her brother / not watch / television
4 he / play / with a computer game
5 what / her father / read?
6 her mother / not / listen to music

H
Do the Module check on page 92.

Language check

THERE IS / THERE ARE

There is / There isn't a supermarket.
There are / There aren't five shops.

SOME / ANY

There are **some** cassettes.
There aren't **any** computer games.
Are there **any** comics?

OBJECT PRONOUNS

My mum takes **me** to school. Does your mum take **you**?
She loves **him** and he loves **her**.
We like **them** but they don't like **us**.

POSSESSIONS

Possessive pronouns
This book is **mine**. That book is **yours**.
This book is **hers**. That book is **his**.
These pens are **ours** and those are **theirs**.

Possessive 's
Whose book is this? It's Sue**'s**.

PRESENT CONTINUOUS

Affirmative
I **am reading** my English book now.
You / We / They **are talking** now.
He / She / It **is watching** TV now.

Negative
I**'m not talking** now.
They**'re not talking** now.

Questions
What **is** he / she / it **doing**?
What **are** you / we / they **doing**?

49

A

Match the words below with the pictures (A–F). Use the mini-dictionary to help you.

horse / dog / tipi / buffalo / knife / arrow

B

Read about the Plains Indians and complete the table below.

Transport	*dogs*
Food	
Weapons	
Homes	
School	
Children's games	

The Plains Indians

1 The Plains Indians didn't live in one place. When they travelled, dogs carried and pulled their things. They didn't use horses. When Spanish people arrived in America, some of 5 their horses escaped. The Indians learned to ride the horses, and used them when they hunted buffaloes.

The Indians cooked the buffalo meat. They used the skins for clothes and shoes. They used 10 the bones for knives and arrows. They lived in *tipis*, tents made of buffalo skins, and they painted them with pictures.

Indians loved their children. Mothers carried babies on their backs. Children didn't go to 15 school! They learned everything from their parents. They played with dolls and had fighting competitions. They played in rivers in the summer and in the snow in the winter.

Life for the Indians changed when Europeans 20 arrived. Standing Bear, an Indian chief, said, 'The plains were not wild for us. Then people arrived from the East and the "Wild West" started.'

F

Language focus: PAST SIMPLE:

AFFIRMATIVE AND NEGATIVE

C

Look at these sentences.

AFFIRMATIVE	NEGATIVE
They **lived** in tipis.	They **didn't live** in one place.

Now copy and complete the table with verbs from the text.

PRESENT SIMPLE	PAST SIMPLE
Affirmative	
live	. . . . .
follow	followed
pull	. . . . .
arrive	. . . . .
carry	. . . . .
Negative	
don't (live)	. . . . .
don't (use)	. . . . .
don't (go)	. . . . .

D

Look at the smoke signals.
Write the verbs in the past simple.

not live

hunt

paint

use

not study

learn

They ¹*hunted* buffaloes.
They ². . . . . in houses.
They ³. . . . . pictures on the tipis.
The children ⁴. . . . . at school.
They ⁵. . . . . skins to make clothes.
They ⁶. . . . . to ride horses.

Pronunciation

E 📼

Listen and repeat these verbs.

1 play**ed** travell**ed** arriv**ed** us**ed**
2 lik**ed** cook**ed** escap**ed** help**ed**
3 hunt**ed** paint**ed** carr**ied** start**ed**

F

Write two true and two false sentences about the Plains Indians. Use these verbs:

play / travel / cook / hunt / use / live

Example: The Indians hunted buffalo. The Indians played computer games.

Now say your sentences. Other students say if they are true or false.

Example: A: The Indians played computer games.
B: False!

51

23 A wild west town

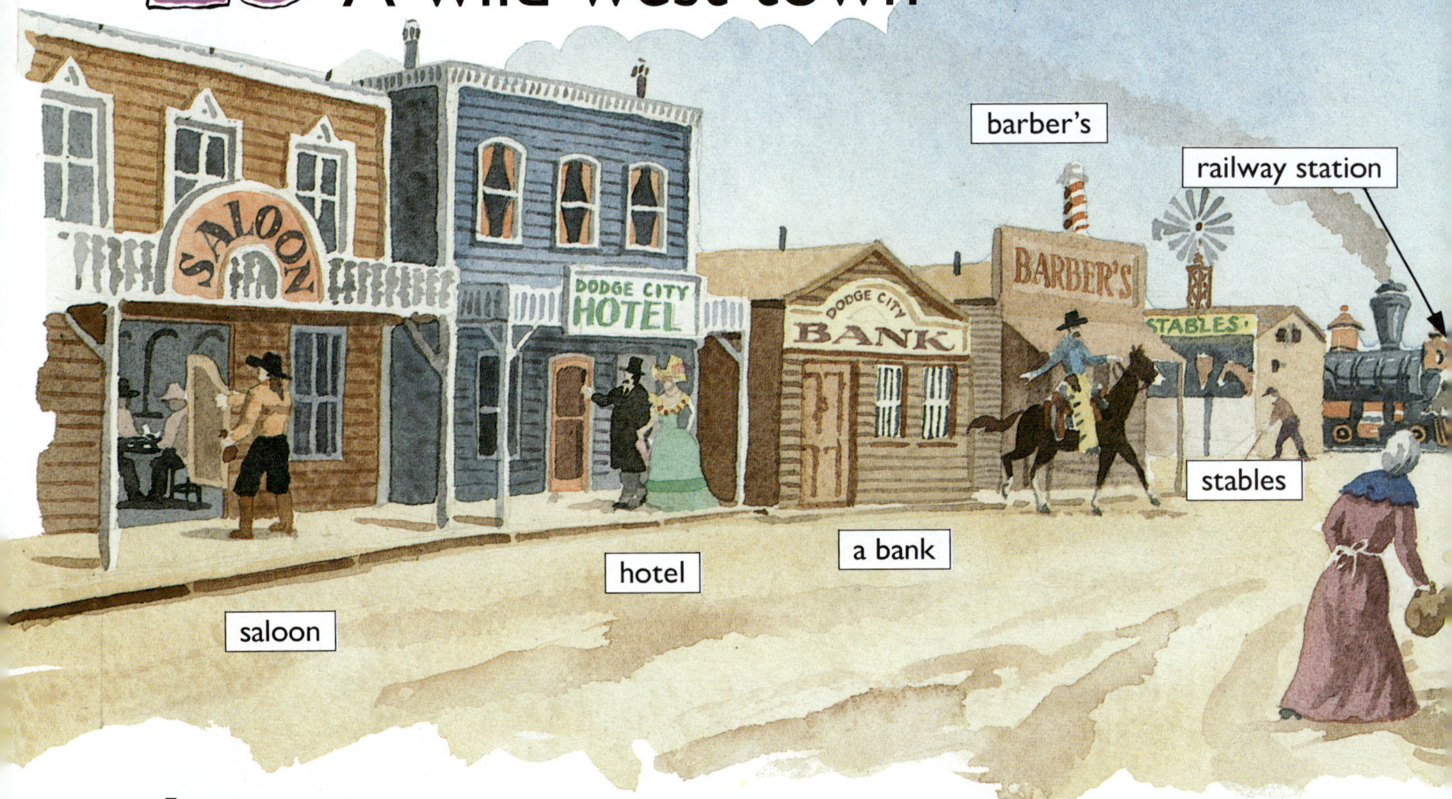

barber's

railway station

stables

a bank

hotel

saloon

A

Look at the picture of the wild west town. In pairs, ask and answer questions. Use these cues:

- to get some money?
- to buy a horse?
- to get a haircut?
- to do some shopping?
- to catch a train?
- to buy a drink?

Example: A: Where do you go to get some money?
B: The bank.

B 📼

Listen to the guide. Number the places on the map in the order she mentions them.

Example: 1 = barber's

RAILWAY STATION

STABLES

GENERAL STORE

SHERIFF'S OFFICE

SALOON

HOTEL

BANK

BARBER'S

sheriff's office

GENERAL STORE

general store

C

Listen and complete the sentences below with these words:

right / left / turn right /
go straight on / turn left

After the barber's, [1] . . . . .
In this street, on the
[2] . . . . . , there is the hotel.
Then in the next street,
[3] . . . . . and the saloon is on
the [4] . . . . . After that,
[5] . . . . . and there are the
stables on the [6] . . . . .

Did you know?

Wyatt Earp was the Sheriff of the most famous of the Wild West towns: Dodge City.

D

Look at the map on page 52 again. Write directions how to get from one place to another.

Example: Start at the hotel. Go straight on. Turn left at the second street . . .

E

In pairs, read your directions from exercise D. Then say 'Where are you?'. If your partner is in the correct place, he/she gets a point.

F

Match the sentences below and join them using *because*.

Example: He went to the barber's *because* he needed a haircut.

1 He went to the barber's   she was rich.
2 She stayed in a hotel   she needed some money.
3 She talked to the sheriff   she had a problem.
4 She visited the bank   he needed a haircut.

G

Team game.

- Make sentences using words coming from your cowboy's gun. You can use a word more than once.
- Take turns to say a sentence.
- The team with the most correct sentences is the winner. The teacher is the referee!

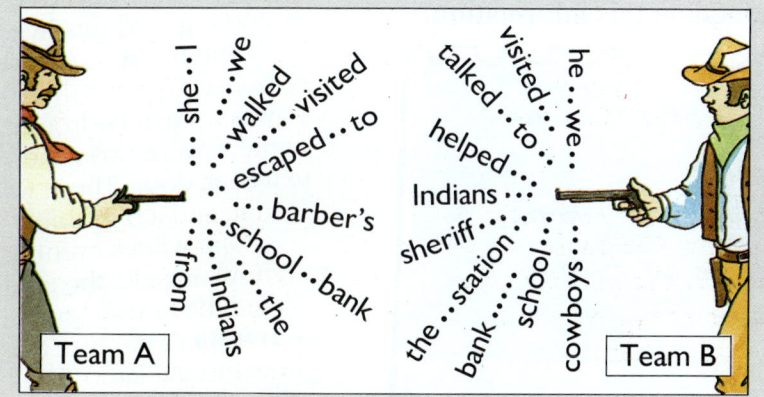

2 indwwo

5 ampl

1 oord

3 reokoc

6 refi

7 baodrupc

4 lebat

8 inrogck aicrh

A

Name the things in the picture.

Example: 1 = door

B

Read about the girl and complete this information.

Name of girl: Laura

House:

Number of rooms:

People in family:

Pets:

Likes:

The little house in the big woods

1 Once upon a time, a girl called Laura lived in a little grey log cabin in the Big Woods of Wisconsin. There weren't any houses and roads and there weren't any people. There were only trees and wild animals. Wolves, bears 5 and big wild cats lived in the Big Woods.

The house wasn't very big, but it was a comfortable house. Upstairs there was an attic and downstairs there was a small bedroom and a big room. In the big room there were two windows and two doors, a front door and 10 a back door. There was a cooker, a cupboard with plates in it, and a big table.

One winter evening, when it was cold and there was snow outside, the family were warm and comfortable in the little house. Laura, her father and her sister Mary were 15 in front of the fire. Her mother was in her rocking chair next to the lamp. The cat and the dog were sleeping in front of the fire. Laura was very happy, she loved her father's stories.

Language focus:

PAST SIMPLE: THE VERB TO BE

C

Look at these examples.
Which are singular and which are plural?

> **AFFIRMATIVE**
>
> There **were** two windows.
> There **was** a cooker.

> **NEGATIVE**
>
> There **weren't** any people.
> The house **wasn't** big.

> **QUESTION**
>
> **Were** they in front of the fire?
> **Was** there a lamp in the room?

D

Complete the sentences with *was* or *were*.

At seven o'clock yesterday, I [1] . . . . . at home. My little sister and I [2] . . . . . in the living room in front of the television. The dog and the cat [3] . . . . . in the garden. My father [4] . . . . . in the kitchen and my mother [5] . . . . . (not) at home. She [6] . . . . . at work. When she returned she asked '[7] . . . . . your little sister good?' 'Yes, she [8] . . . . .', I said.

> ## Did you know?
>
> Laura Ingalls Wilder started to write The 'Little House' books in 1932. They are true stories about her family.

Pronunciation

E

Listen and write the sentences. Then count the words.

Example: 1 I was at school. = 4 words

(words numbered above: I[1] was[2] at[3] school[4])

Listen again and repeat the sentences.

F

In pairs, ask questions about where your partner was at these times yesterday.

- 6 o'clock in the morning
- 9 o'clock in the morning
- 2 o'clock in the afternoon
- 7 o'clock in the evening
- 11 o'clock at night

> Where were you at 6 o'clock in the morning?

> I was at home, in bed!

G

Memory game.

- In groups, close your books. What can you remember about the room in the log cabin?

>  There were two windows.

> There was a fire.

- When you can't remember, you are out of the game.

25 Television

westerns

nature programmes

cartoons

sports programmes

comedies

music programmes

BBC 1

5.30
Cartoon Time:
Some classic Disney

6.00
News and Weather

6.15
Alias Smith and Jones:
More cowboy
adventures

7.00
The Video Show:
Pop music videos

7.30
Football:
England v Holland, from
Wembley

BBC 2

7.00
Underwater World:
This week's nature
programme looks at
sharks

8.00
Dances with Wolves:
The fantastic Hollywood
western with Kevin
Costner

ITV

5.15
The Game Kids:
Teams of children play
computer games

5.45
News and Weather

6.00
**Little House in the Big
Woods:**
Another episode in the
life of Laura

6.45
Win a Million!
The quiz show with big
prizes

7.15
Smile, Please:
Another funny selection
of your own videos

CHANNEL 4

8.00
Comedy Classics:
This week: Charlie
Chaplin

8.45
Prince:
His last UK Tour

A

In groups, look at the televisions on page 56 and say what types of programmes you like. Then tell the class which programmes are popular in your group.

Example: Paul likes westerns, Ali and Nicole like comedies and I like sports programmes.

B

Now look at the TV page on page 56. Which programmes are westerns?

Example: Dances with Wolves

C

Look at the TV page again. Match the channel and time with the type of programme.

Example: 1 BBC 1, 5.30 = cartoons

1 BBC 1, 5.30
2 BBC 1, 7.00
3 BBC 1, 7.30
4 BBC 2, 7.00
5 BBC 2, 8.00
6 ITV, 7.15
7 Channel 4, 8.00

D 📼

Listen to Claire and Peter. What do they think about the programmes? Copy and complete the table with these words.

boring / quite good / interesting / funny / exciting / brilliant

Programme	Claire	Peter
1 Underwater World	. . . . .	quite good
2 Football	. . . . .	. . . . .
3 Prince	. . . . .	. . . . .
4 Smile, Please	. . . . .	. . . . .

E

Choose three programmes you want to watch. In groups, say what you want to watch and give your opinions. Use the words from exercise D.

Example: A: I want to watch *Underwater World*.
B: Yes, I think nature programmes are brilliant.
C: I think they're boring.
D: I agree, they're boring.

Choose one programme that everybody in your group wants to watch. Tell the class.

Example: We want to watch *Dances with Wolves*.

Did you know?

Real cowboys were not as tall as they are in films. Most of them were small men.

 **Annie Oakley**

The story in six pictures labeled A–F.

A

Listen to the life story of Annie Oakley. Put the pictures in the correct order.

Example: 1 = E

Language focus 1: PAST SIMPLE WH-QUESTIONS

B

Listen and match the questions with the answers.

Questions	*Answers*
Where did they travel?	a) She performed incredible tricks.
What did Annie do?	b) In 1926.
When did she die?	c) Around America and Europe.

C

Write questions about Annie Oakley. Use *did* and the words below.

Example: 1 When did she start using guns?

1 when / she start using guns?
2 who / she marry?
3 when / she have train accident?
4 where / she die?

Language focus 2:

PAST SIMPLE YES / NO QUESTIONS

D

Look at the examples in the boxes.

QUESTIONS
Did she **come** from a rich family? **Did** she **win** the competition?

SHORT ANSWERS
No, she **didn't**. Yes, she **did**.

Write questions and answers about Annie. Use *did* and the words below.

Example: 1 Did she win the competition?
                Yes, she did.

1 win the competition?
2 live in a big house?
3 travel a lot?
4 have a bad accident?

E

In pairs, ask and answer the questions below. Give *one* false answer. At the end, your partner guesses what was false.

★ Your life ★

1 When did you start learning English?
2 Did you enjoy your first day at school?
3 What did you see on your first visit to the cinema?
4 Where did you go on your first holiday?
5 What games did you play when you were five years old?
6 Who did you play with when you were five?
7 Did you buy any new toys last year?
8 When did you learn to swim?
9 What present did you get for your birthday last year?
10 When did you buy your first CD or cassette? What was it?

Tell the class about your partner.

Example: Sofia started learning English when she was eight years old!

Did you know?

Annie Oakley could shoot a coin or the thin edge of a playing card from 30 metres!

27 Fluency

A
LEARN TO LEARN
When do you hear English?

- in the classroom
- on the radio
- in pop songs
- on holiday
- in films and videos
- on television
- tourists in your town

B
Listen to the song and fill in the gaps.

Billy the Kid

This is a song about Billy the Kid,
This is the story of things that he ^{1}.....
In the wild west a long time ago
He ^{2}..... and he died down in old Mexico.

Billy the Kid, Billy the Kid! Poor Billy the Kid!

Pat Garrett, the Sheriff ^{3}..... Billy the Kid,
But he put him in prison for the things that he did.
But Billy ^{4}..... and started to run
He said, "No-one can catch me now, I'm number one!"

Billy the Kid, Billy the Kid! Poor Billy the Kid!

Now on the sad night when poor Billy ^{5}.....,
He said to his friends I'm not satisfied,
Twenty-one men I ^{6}..... that it true,
Now Sheriff Pat Garrett is number twenty-two.

Billy the Kid, Billy the Kid! Poor Billy the Kid.

Now this is how Billy's life came to an end,
He ^{7}..... one night at the house of a friend.
Pat Garrett ^{8}..... in, saw Billy in bed,
He pulled out his gun and poor Billy was dead.

Billy the Kid, Billy the Kid! Poor Billy the Kid.
Billy the Kid, Billy the Kid! Poor Billy the Kid.

C
Look at the picture of Billy the Kid and read the description on the poster. Find six mistakes in the description.

Example: His face is fat, not thin.

WANTED
DEAD OR ALIVE

BILLY THE KID

Billy the Kid is young but very dangerous. His face is thin and his hair is short and dark. His eyes are brown and his nose is small. He wears a white hat and a yellow scarf.

Reward: $5,000

D

Think of three television programmes you watched last week. In pairs, tell your partner about them.

Example: A: On Saturday, I watched the Bugs Bunny Show. It was really funny.

B: I didn't see that. I watched a Clint Eastwood film. He was a cowboy. It was brilliant.

A: I watched that. It was quite good. On Monday I watched . . .

E

Draw a street plan of the your area where you live.

- In pairs, give your partner the plan.
- Then give him/her directions to your house. He/She marks the route on the plan.
- Check your partner's route.

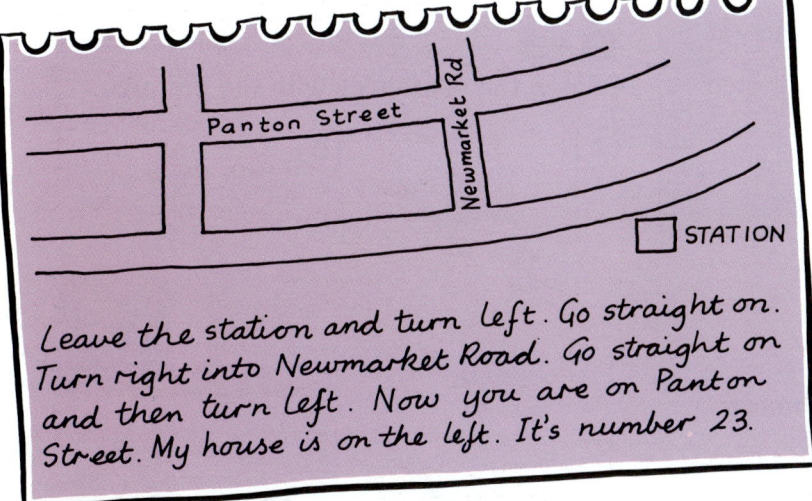

Leave the station and turn left. Go straight on. Turn right into Newmarket Road. Go straight on and then turn left. Now you are on Panton Street. My house is on the left. It's number 23.

Learner training

F

Match the grammar words on the left with the examples on the right.

1 affirmative   a) Did you see that film?
2 negative   b) child
3 question   c) They live in tipis.
4 singular   d) children
5 plural   e) We didn't go out.

Project

G

Make a wanted poster.

1 Think of a name for the person.

2 Write notes about size / hair / eyes / nose / clothes.

tall and dangerous

hair - long and black

3 Write a description.

She is tall and dangerous.

Her hair is long and black.

4 Check the description for mistakes.

5 Draw a picture and write your description neatly.

28 Language revision

Language practice

A

Team game.

- Play in two teams: Team O and Team X.
- Take turns to choose a box.
- Say a sentence with the verb in the past (affirmative, negative or question).

  Example: **I didn't go** on holiday.

- If the sentence is correct, put O or X in that box.
- You win when you complete a line.

not go	live	not study
escape	play?	carry
listen?	paint	not watch

- Now choose different verbs and play the game in pairs.

Vocabulary

B

Where are these things in your house?

knives / food / television / clothes / plates / bed / table / cupboards / posters / sofa / books / radio / telephone

Copy and complete the networks.

In pairs, compare your lists. Are there any differences?

C

Word game.

- All the students in the class take turns to say a word.
- You say a word which begins with the *last* letter of the word before you.

  Example: A: appl**e**
  B: **ex**am
  C: **m**eat
  D: **ta**ke
  E: **e**gg
  F: **g** . . . . .

- If you can't think of a word, you are out of the game.

D

Match the sentences with the pictures.

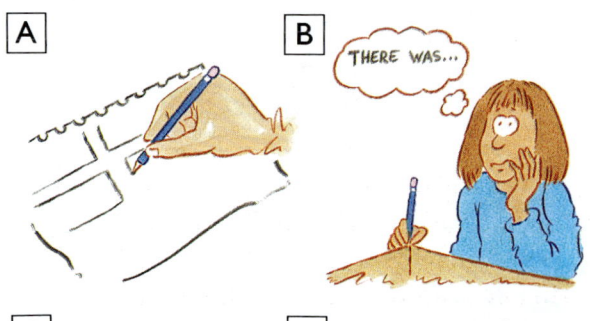

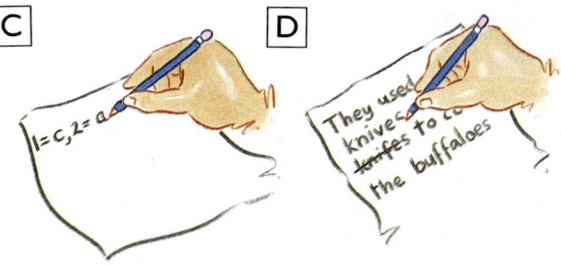

1 What can you remember about the picture?
2 Draw a plan of the town.
3 Put the pictures in order.
4 Check your description for mistakes.

Pronunciation

E 📼

Listen to the words. Mark the stress.

Example: anim□al   esc□ape

animal / escape / popular / hotel / accident /
cupboard / arrow / Indian

Listen again and repeat the words.

Test yourself

F

Put the verbs in the past tense.

Cynthia-Ann Parker (be) [1] . . . . . a young
American girl. She (live) [2] . . . . . with her
family at Parker's Fort in Texas. In 1836 the
Comanche Indians (attack) [3] . . . . . their
farm and (capture) [4] . . . . . the nine-year-old
Cynthia-Ann.

   Cynthia-Ann (learn) [5] . . . . . the
Comanche language and (be) [6] . . . . .
happy. She (marry) [7] . . . . . a Comanche
chief called Peta Noconi. One day the US
Army (arrive) [8] . . . . . at the Comanche
village and (discover) [9] . . . . . a woman with
blue eyes and blonde hair – Cynthia-Anne.
She returned with the Army.

   But Cynthia (not want) [10] . . . . . to live
with her own people. She (not like) [11] . . . . .
the houses, the food or the people. She (be
not) [12] . . . . . happy and after a few years she
(die) [13] . . . . . .

Language check

PAST SIMPLE: AFFIRMATIVE / NEGATIVE

Affirmative
They **lived** in tents.
Dogs **carried** their things.

Negative
They **didn't live** in houses.
They **didn't use** horses.

PAST SIMPLE: THE VERB TO BE

Affirmative
There **was** a cooker.
There **were** two windows.

Negative
The house **wasn't** very big.
There **weren't** any horses.

PAST SIMPLE: QUESTIONS

Yes/No questions
Did they **live** in houses?
Yes, they **did**./No, they **didn't**.

Wh- questions
When did she die?
What did they eat?
Where did they live?

G

**Write questions for these answers about
Cynthia-Ann Parker.**

Example: 1 Where did she live?

1 At Parker's Fort in Texas.
2 She was nine.
3 She married Peta Noconi.
4 No, she wasn't happy.

H 🔲LEARN TO LEARN

Now do the Module check on page 92.

29 Getting to school

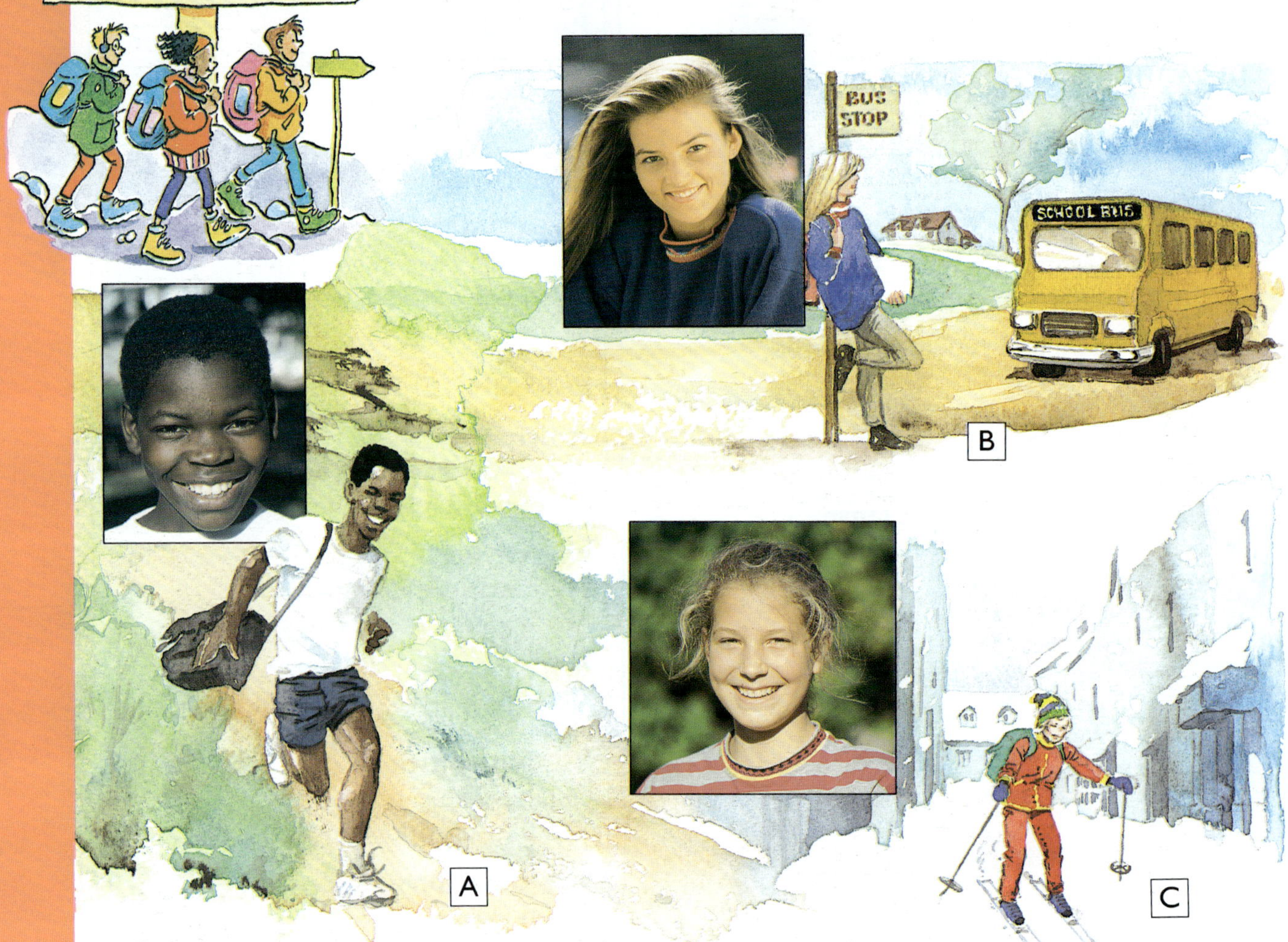

A
Match the sentences with the pictures.

1 Mary-Jo Wilson goes to school by bus.
2 Nixon Ouko runs to school.
3 Mikaela Harfaager goes to school on skis.

B 🖭
Where do you think the people in exercise A live?
Listen and write the names of their countries.

Language focus:
PREPOSITIONS: IN / ON / AT / BY

C 🖭
Listen again and complete the sentences below with the prepositions.

in / on / at / by

1 I go to school . . . . . bus.
2 I leave home . . . . . eight o'clock.
3 I go to school . . . . . foot.
4 . . . . . the winter I go . . . . . skis.
5 . . . . . Saturdays I go . . . . . car with my dad.
6 Do you have school . . . . . the weekend?
7 We have school . . . . . the morning . . . . . Saturdays.

D

What preposition do we use with the words below? Copy and complete the table.

8 o'clock / the morning / Monday / the weekend / bus / 21st March / foot / night / the afternoon / winter / bicycle / skis / 1994

at	*8 o'clock*
in	*the morning*
on	
by	

E

Complete the description with *at, in, on, by*.

My name is Nikos and I live [1]. . . . . a small town. I get up [2]. . . . . seven o'clock [3]. . . . . the morning and I leave the house [4]. . . . . half past seven. I go to school [5]. . . . . bicycle. We don't have school [6]. . . . . the weekend. [7]. . . . . Saturdays my friends and I go out on our bicycles, but on Sundays I go to church with my mother – [8]. . . . . foot!

Pronunciation

F 📼

Listen and repeat the times.

seven o'clock

half past seven

quarter past seven

quarter to eight

eight o'clock

G 💬

In groups, ask and answer these questions.

- How do you get to school?
- What time do you get up?

Write the answers in your notebook.

H

In pairs, collect the information from exercise G and draw a graph.

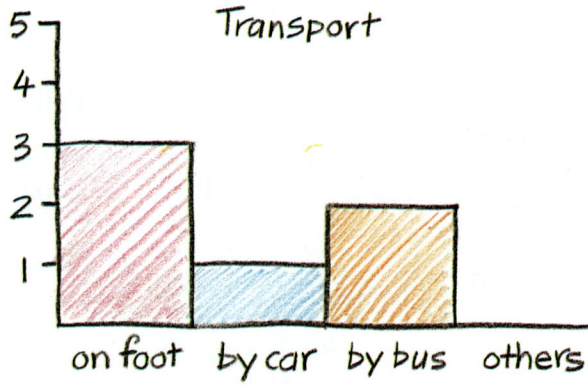

30 Holidays

seaside holiday

pleasure park

touring holiday

adventure holiday

AQUA PARK

Fun for all the family in our indoor, heated, 25 metre pool! Plus . . .

Aquapark is open 7 days a week
from 7.00 am – 10.00 pm.
Telephone: 063 94 81

A

Look at the photos above and give each holiday a 'fun' score.

Key for individual scores	
1 = boring	3 = good fun
2 = OK	4 = brilliant

B

In groups of four, add up the scores. Tell the results to the class.

Example: We think seaside holidays are good
fun.

Key for group scores	
1–4 = boring	9–12 = good fun
5–8 = OK	13–16 = brilliant

C

Read the text about *Aquapark* and give it a 'fun' score.

D

Read the text again. True or false?

1 The water is warm.
2 There is a pool for young children.
3 There is a disco-pool every night.
4 Bad swimmers can use the Magic Tube.
5 Aquapark is closed on Mondays.

Poolside bar and restaurant a great place to relax after your swim!

The Fast River* sail down the rapids on a small boat!

Disco-pool with music and lights – every Friday and Saturday.

Mini-pool with toys for small children.

The Magic Tube* enter the pool with a big splash!

*These are only for good swimmers.

E 📼

Listen to the phone conversation and complete the dialogue.

WOMAN: Aquapark, good morning.
GIRL: Hello [1] . . . . . does Aquapark close today?
WOMAN: We close at ten o'clock every night.
GIRL: [2] . . . . . is it, please?
WOMAN: Tickets are [3] . . . . . pounds for [4] . . . . . hours.
GIRL: Thanks very much. Bye.
WOMAN: Goodbye.

F 〰️

In pairs, practise the dialogue in exercise E. Change the price and the times.

31 Airships

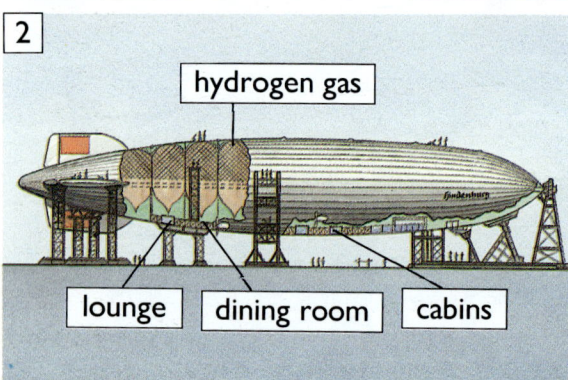

hydrogen gas

lounge | dining room | cabins

A

Match the pictures with paragraphs A, B, C and D.

Example: A = 2

B

Read the text and answer these questions.

1 When did the *Hindenburg* leave Germany?
2 How long did it take to get to America.
3 Where did it explode?

The Hindenburg

A The Zeppelin company made enormous airships. The airships only took two days to go from Europe to America. In 1929 an airship called the Graf Zeppelin went around the world in twenty-one days!

B On 4th May 1937, another airship called the *Hindenburg*, left Germany to cross the Atlantic. It had thirty-five passengers on board.

C The passengers on the *Hindenburg* were very comfortable. They slept in cabins, sat and played cards in a lounge, and ate and drank in a big dining room. In the evenings they listened to music from a grand piano and danced!

D On 6th May the *Hindenburg* arrived in New Jersey, but the people did not get to their destination. Suddenly the airship exploded! All the people died.

Language focus:

PAST SIMPLE: IRREGULAR VERBS

C

Find the past tense of these verbs in the text on page 68.

make / take / go / leave / has / are / sleep / sit / eat / drink

D

Look at the verbs *play* and *leave* in the boxes. Which one is irregular?

AFFIRMATIVE

They **played** cards.
The Hindenburg **left** on 4th May.

NEGATIVE

They **didn't play** tennis.
It **didn't leave** on 3rd May.

QUESTIONS

Did they **play** cards?
Did it **leave** on 4th May?

Did you know?

In 1783 Jacques Charles Cesar made the first hydrogen balloon.

E

Put the verbs in the text below in the past simple. There is a list of irregular verbs on page 93.

Example: 1 = left

> Around the world in an airship
> We 1_____(leave) Germany in the airship on May 21st.
> There 2_____(are) twenty passengers.
> In the evening we 3_____(have) a fantastic dinner and we 4_____(listen) to music. I 5_____(not sleep) very well. The next day I 6_____(get up) late and I 7_____(not eat) breakfast.
> In the afternoon I 8_____(sit) in the lounge and 9_____(play) cards. In the evening there 10_____(is) a party.
> Two days later, we 11_____(arrive) in Japan.

F

In groups, ask and answer questions about a journey you made.

- Where did you go?
- What time did you get up?
- What did you eat for breakfast?
- What time did you leave home?
- How did you travel?
- What did you do in the afternoon / evening?
- What time did you go to bed?

G

One person from the group tells the class about a journey.

Example: Silvia went to the seaside. She got up at . . .

69

32 Father and son

The Adventures of Eric and Leif

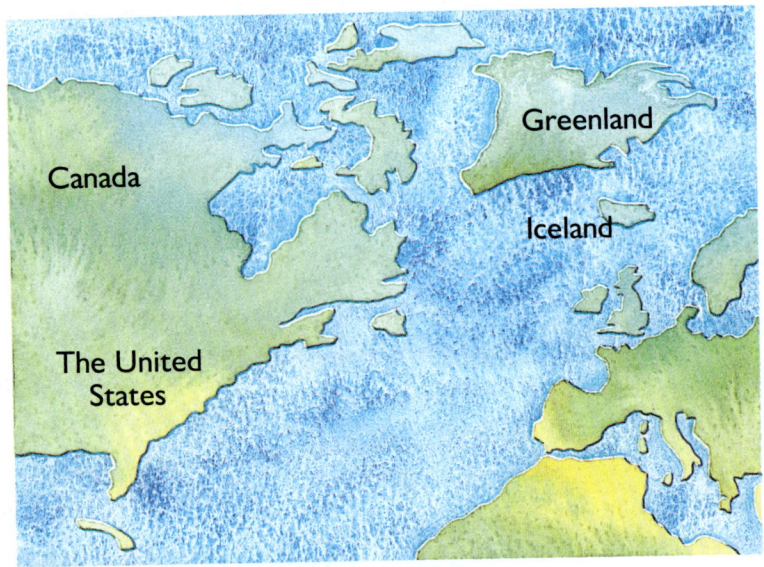

1 Eric the Red was born in Norway in about 950, but he moved to Iceland with his father when he was a boy.

5 When he was a young man, people called him 'the Red' because of his red hair. Eric had many enemies and he killed two men. He decided to

10 leave Iceland to escape his enemies.

In 982 Eric and some of his friends sailed west and found a new country. It was cold and

15 white because of the snow, but Eric wanted people to come to his country, so he called it 'Greenland'. He

returned to Iceland and told
20 people that Greenland was
very beautiful. He sailed back
to Greenland in 986, with
people who wanted to live
there. The ships were very
25 small (24 metres long), but
they took with them cows,
pigs, hens and sheep.

Leif, Eric's son, was born in
about 975 and went to live
30 with his father in Greenland.
He was tall and strong and
people called him 'Leif the
Lucky' because he had very
good luck. Like his father he
35 was adventurous and wanted
to travel.

In 1002 Leif sailed west to
look for another new country
that sailors talked about. First,
40 he found a place which he
called 'Markland' (now called
Labrador, in Canada). There
were many trees, and rivers
with salmon in them. The
45 expedition went south and
came to a green and beautiful
place. They found vines and
grapes so Leif called the
country 'Vinland' (now the
50 north of the United States).
Leif and his men were
probably the first Europeans
in America!

A

Look at the drawings on page 70 and match them with the countries on the map.

Example: D = Canada

Now read about Eric the Red and his son Leif and check your answers. Read the text again and order the pictures.

B

Look at the time line below and read the text again. Match the sentences with the years.

Example: 950 = Eric was born.

- A big expedition went to Greenland.
- Leif went to America.
- Eric left Iceland.
- Eric was born.
- Leif was born.

—1——	—2——	—3——	—4——	—5—
950	975	982	986	1002

C

Write notes about your life.

1984 – born
1988 – went to school
1990 – holiday in America
1993 – started English classes

D

In pairs, give your notes to your partner. Write a biography of your partner.

Example: Sandra was born in 1983. She went to school in 1987 and then . . .

Pronunciation

E

Listen to the pronunciation of these years.

1002 = ten-oh-two
1994 = nineteen-ninety-four

Now listen and write the years you hear.

Example: 1 = 1995

Listen again and repeat the years.

F

Guessing game.

- In groups, exchange your biographies from exercise D.
- Read a biography and the others guess who it is.

This person was born in 1984 . . .

33 Gulliver's travels

A

Listen to the story and put the pictures in order.

Example: 1 = B

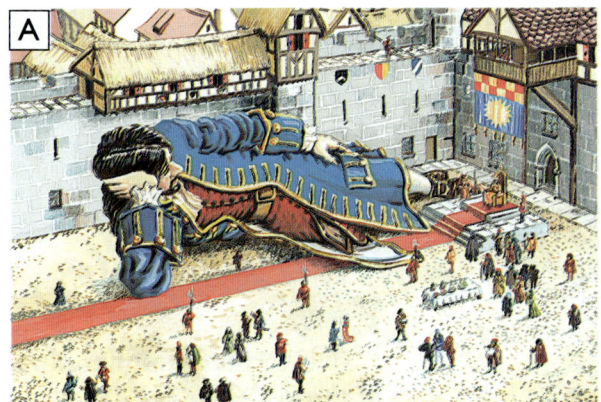

Language focus:
COUNTABLES AND UNCOUNTABLES

B

Look at picture E. Which things can you count and make plural?

Example: one chicken, two chickens ✓
one rice, two rice ✗

Put the words from the picture under the correct heading. Countable or Uncountable?

Example: Countable – chicken
Uncountable – rice

C

Listen to Gulliver again. Copy and complete the tables with *some* or *any*.

AFFIRMATIVE		
There is	.....	water.
There are		chickens.

NEGATIVE		
There isn't	.....	milk.
There aren't		tomatoes.

QUESTIONS		
Is there	.....	cheese?
Are there		potatoes?

SHORT ANSWERS
Yes, there is.
No, there isn't.
Yes, there are.
No, there aren't.

1 Do we use *is* or *are* for countables and uncountables?
2 Do we use *some* or *any* in affirmative sentences?
3 Do we use *some* or *any* in negative sentences?
4 Do we use *some* or *any* in questions?

How do you say the sentences in the boxes in your language?

D
Look at picture E again. Write sentences using these words.

oranges / rice / apples / bread / carrots / sugar / cheese / eggs

Example: There aren't any oranges.
There is some rice.

E

Write down five things to eat and drink. In pairs, ask your partner questions and find out what's for dinner. The one who finds out the five things first is the winner.

Are there any potatoes?

Yes, there are. Is there any cheese?

No, there isn't. Is there . . . ?

F

In pairs, look at picture E again for 30 seconds. Then close your books. Test your partner.

Example: A: How many plates of rice are there?
B: Six.
A: Wrong! Seven.

A

Read the poem. Which words do you think go in the gaps? Listen and see if you were correct.

Example: 1 = sail
2 = boat

Off we go!

Let's ^{1}. . . . . away in a ^{2}. . . . .
Don't forget to take your coat!

Let's ^{3}. . . . . away on a ^{4}. . . . .
And take some lemonade of course!

Let's ^{5}. . . . . away in a ^{6}. . . . .
We can go ever so far!

Let's ^{7}. . . . . away in a ^{8}. . . . .
We can go all the way to Spain!

Let's ^{9}. . . . . away in a balloon
And have a nice afternoon!

Let's go away on a ^{10}. . . . .
And never come back again!

B

Holiday survey: what do you take on holiday?

- Write a list of five important things you take on holiday.
- Ask the others in your class about their lists.

Example: A: What do you take?
B: A camera, a computer game, a ball, my swimming costume, and some cassettes.

- Make a graph of the five important things your class takes on holiday.

C

Listen to five children talking about their holidays. Did they think the holidays were good or bad?

Example: 1 = good

D

Fill in the gaps with *a, an, the*.

Example: 1 We got on **a** plane. **The** plane took us to Portugal.

1 We got on . . . . . plane. . . . . . plane took us to Portugal.
2 My sister sat next to . . . . . boy. . . . . . boy was Portuguese.
3 I talked to . . . . . air hostess. . . . . . air hostess was kind.
4 We stayed in . . . . . hotel. . . . . . hotel was great.

E

Now change the second sentence in each example in exercise D. Use *he, she, it*.

Example: 1 **It** took us to Portugal.

F

LEARN TO LEARN

Look at the reading activities in Modules 1 to 5. Choose your three favourite readings.

Project

G

In pairs, write an adventure story.

1 Invent a character who went to a strange place.

2 Write notes about his/her journey and who he/she meets.

> - plane crash
> - Shera alone on island
> - builds house
> - sees strange animals
> - frightened
> - meets people in village
> - builds boat
> - leaves island

3 Use your notes to write the story. Check it for mistakes.

> Shera got up ~~at~~ *in* the morning. She decided to build a house ~~at~~ *on* the be~~a~~ch... suddenly, in the river, she ~~see~~ *saw* a giant fish ...

4 Draw a map and illustrate the story.

35 Language revision

	Silvia	Kate	Nicola	Maria	Fatima	Eva	Lola
Get up							
Go							
Take							
Eat							
Drink							
Arrive							
Stay							

Language practice

A

In pairs, look at the table above. Student A talks about a girl's holiday. Student B guesses who it is. You get a point if you are correct.

Example: A: She got up at 7.15. She went by train. She took three bags.

B: Lola. (Correct! One point)

B [LEARN TO LEARN]

In pairs, find five words in this module that are difficult to spell. Then test your partner.

Example: A: How do you spell *restaurant*?

B: R–E–S–T–A–U–R–A–N–T.

Vocabulary

C

Team game.

- Write the name of an object from this module on a piece of paper.
- The teacher collects the pieces of paper.
- One student from Team A chooses a piece of paper and draws the object on the board.
- The other students from Team A guess what the object is. They have three guesses.
- If they guess the object, they get a point.
- Then Team B has a turn.

Pronunciation

D

Listen to these words.

Group 1 — day

Group 2 — bike

Put these words into the correct group.

train / plane / night / came / time / died / take / rice / stayed

Listen again and repeat the words.

Test yourself

E

Complete the text with the past simple of these verbs.

go / write / leave / not like / travel / not return / is / are / die

Lady Hester Stanhope [1] *was* born in Britain in 1776. When she was thirty-four, she [2] . . . . . to live in Istanbul. After two years she [3] . . . . . Istanbul to go to Cairo. From Cairo she [4] . . . . . to Palestine and the Syrian desert. The Druze people in the desert [5] . . . . . strangers, but they [6] . . . . . friendly to Lady Hester. After that she [7] . . . . . about her travels. She [8] . . . . . to Britain and she [9] . . . . . in the Lebanon in 1839.

F

Complete Lady Hester's diary with these words.

by / at / on / in

We travelled [1] *by* camel and, [2] . . . . . 20th May, we arrived at the old city of Palmyra. [3] . . . . . night it was cold and I did not sleep well. I got up [4] . . . . . 5.30 am. [5] . . . . . the morning we walked around the old city [6] . . . . . foot.

G [LEARN TO LEARN]

Now do the Module check on page 92.

36 Galactic tours

A

Look at this alien. What is funny about her?

Example: She's got four arms.

Now look at the big picture. What are the aliens doing?

B

Listen to the guide. Which of these things do the aliens think are funny about us?

1 We've got two eyes.
2 We've got two legs and two arms.
3 We live in small houses.
4 We watch television.
5 We sleep for eight hours a day.
6 Children stay at school for six hours.

head
ears
mouth
arm
leg

Language focus: PRESENT SIMPLE / PRESENT CONTINUOUS

C

Listen to these sentences again and put the verbs in the correct tense.

Example: 1 = *wear* (present simple)

1 They (wear) very strange clothes.
2 They (eat) fruit and vegetables.
3 Now, the people (go) to work.
4 At the moment it (rain).
5 The children (go) to school by bus.
6 People (like) parks.

What are sentences 1 and 4 in your language?
Look at the sentences in the box.

> They **wear** very strange clothes.
> At the moment it **is raining**.

In which sentence is something happening *now*? In which sentence does something happen all the time?

D

Read the information below about Zorgons. Are they the same as you?

Example: I don't eat rocks. I eat fruit and vegetables.

> ### The Zorgons
>
> Zorgons eat rocks and drink petrol.
> Zorgons wear white clothes.
> Zorgons live on the planet Zorg.
> Zorgons sleep for one hour a day.

E

Look at the picture. What are the Zorgons doing *now*?

Example: Zeeta is playing a computer game.

F

Invent your own aliens. First think of these things:

- where they live
- food
- clothes
- hobbies

In pairs, describe your alien to your partner. Your partner draws it.

> It has got three eyes and two noses. It has got three arms and four legs.

When you finish, look at your partner's picture. Is it similar to yours?

37 World quiz

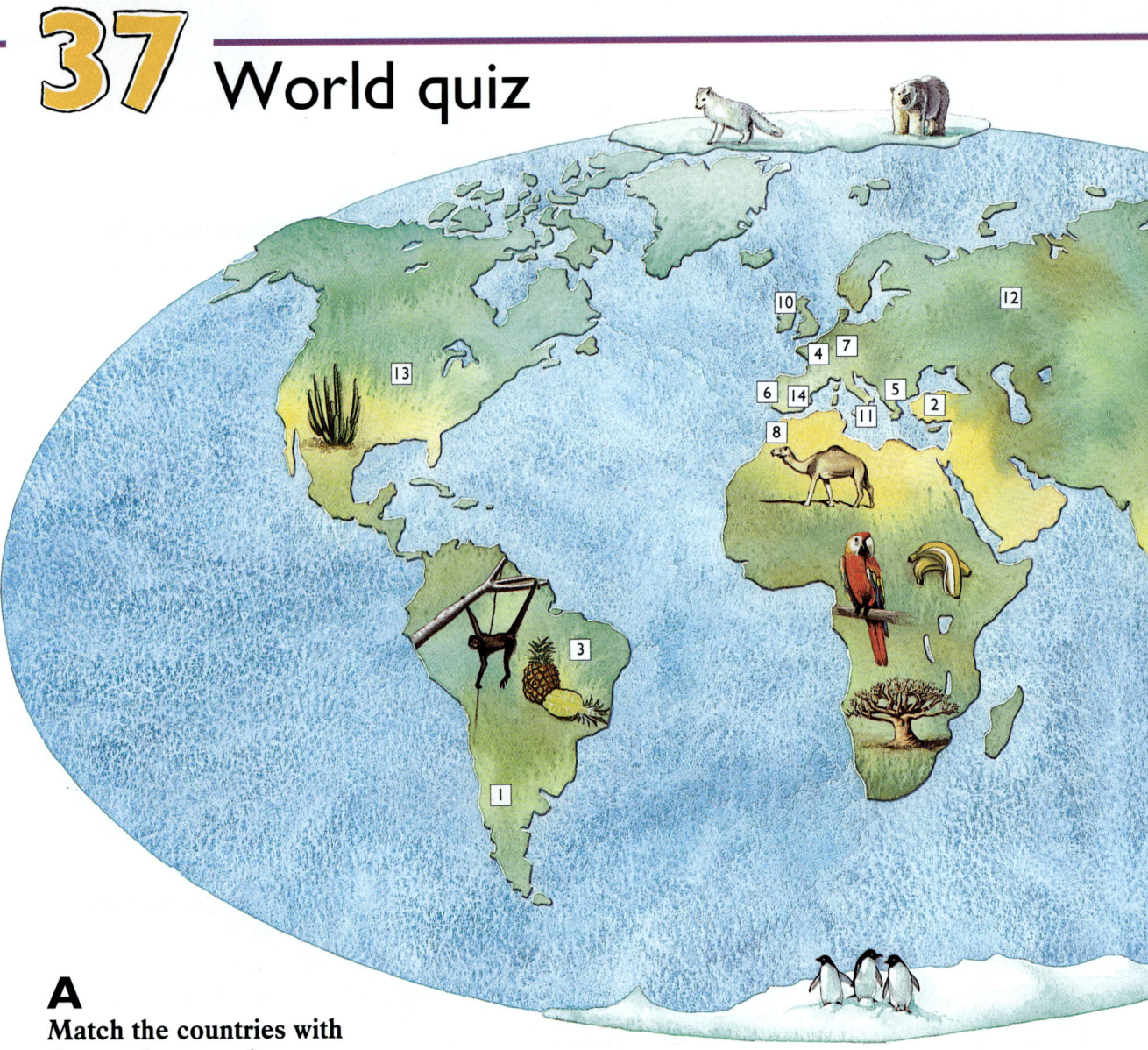

A

Match the countries with the numbers on the map.

Example: 1 = Argentina

Portugal / Italy / Greece / Brazil / China / Britain / Germany / Argentina / Morocco / Japan / Turkey / United States / Spain / France / Russia

Where is your country on the map?

B

In pairs, try to complete the information on the computer. Use an atlas to help you.

Example: Continents = Europe / South America / North America

Name of planet: Earth
Surface: 29% land 71% water
Continents: Asia / Africa / Australia / Antarctica / . . . . .
Oceans: . . . . . / Indian / Arctic
Mountains: . . . . . Everest (8,848 m) Andes: (Aconagua 6,960 m)
Rivers: . . . . . / Mississippi / Congo
Population: 7 billion
Languages: 4000 different languages

C

Listen to the quiz and write down the answers to the questions. In groups, compare your answers. Report the answers to the class.

Now listen to the answers to the quiz. The group with the most correct answers is the winner!

D

In pairs, write six questions. Use the information in exercise B and the map to help you.

Example: What is the capital of Spain?

E

In groups of four (two pairs), close your books then ask and answer the questions. (A correct answer = two points.)

Pronunciation

F

Look at the list of countries on page 93. Copy the first seven countries. Listen and mark the stress.

Example: 1 Morŏcco / Morŏccan   2 Eŭrope/Europeăn

Listen again and repeat the words.

G

Look at these notes about a country. What country is it?

Flag: 🇦🇺   Population: 16 million
Capital: Canberra
Rivers: Murray River
Mountains: Snowy Mountains
Languages: English/Aborigine language

Write notes about *your* country.

Did you know?

Planet Earth is 29% land and 71% water.

SEA

LAND

38 Meeting humans

A

Answer this questionnaire.

Meeting people

1 **When you meet somebody new, what do you do?**
a) kiss them
b) shake hands
c) say 'hello'

2 **When somebody is talking to you, what do you do?**
a) look at them
b) close your eyes
c) read a book

3 **When you visit somebody's house, what do you do?**
a) turn on the TV and watch it
b) say nice things about their house
c) read their letters

B

In pairs, which of the things in the questionnaire are very bad to do in your country? Report your answers to the rest of the class.

Did you know?

In films some aliens are friendly (ET) and some, like 'Alien', are not!

C

Read the Zorgon guide to humans. Find three examples of bad advice.

● Advice for Zorgon visitors ●
● PLANET EARTH ●

♦ When you meet a human, smile and say 'Hello. Don't worry, I am not dangerous. I am a visitor to your planet.'
♦ When you visit a human's house, sit on the ceiling.
♦ When a human gives you food, say: 'Thank you very much, but I eat rocks.'
♦ When you want to do something, say: 'Let's watch television.' 'Why don't we play tennis?' or 'What about going to the cinema?'
♦ When the human is talking, close your eyes.
♦ Say nasty things about the planet: 'There's a horrible smell on this planet.'
♦ Don't give the human a Zorgon kiss. (This is very dangerous.)

Language focus: SUGGESTIONS

D 📼

Listen to the conversation between a Zorgon and a human. Match the suggestions (1 to 3) to the replies (a to c).

1 **Let's** play dominoes.
2 **Why don't we** go the park?
3 **What about** having lunch?

a) Okay, let's do that.
b) That's a good idea!
c) No, thanks.

E

In pairs, student A suggests four of the activities below. Student B replies. Then student B suggests four activities and student A replies.

go to the cinema / play football / play table tennis / watch a video / make a model / go to the shops / go swimming / have a sandwich

F

Write five suggestions for this weekend.

Example: Why don't we go to a football match on Saturday?

G

In groups, copy the diary below. Then suggest activities to the others.

Friday
shopping, Sylvia, 4 p.m.
_____
Saturday
_____
Sunday
_____

 Why don't we go swimming on Saturday afternoon?

No, thanks.

 What about going to the shops on Friday afternoon?

Okay.

Write the activities in your diary.

 **The living planet**

A

Choose the words to describe the photos.

Example: tropical forest = hot

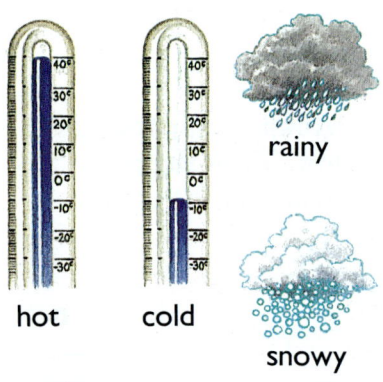

hot   cold

rainy

snowy

icy   sunny   dry

B

Read the travel information and check your answers to exercise A.

Did you know?

There are about 10 million kinds of animals and plants on our planet, but fifty disappear every day!

EARTH
The Living Planet

Fantastic forests

Go to the hot, rainy tropical forests of Africa or South America. There are trees sixty metres tall and a lot of tropical fruits like bananas and pineapples. There is also a lot of animal life: gorillas, leopards, monkeys, parrots and thousands of kinds of insects.

Cold poles

When you go to the Arctic, wear warm clothes! Here it is very cold, with temperatures of −80°C and it is snowy and icy all the year. You can see polar bears and beautiful arctic foxes. And in the Antarctic there are funny birds called penguins.

Visit this small but curious planet. But go NOW! A lot of plants and animals are disappearing.

Hot spots

In the deserts it is very dry, hot and sunny, with temperatures up to 57°C. There are plants here called cactuses that can live with very little water, and there are some curious animals: kangaroos, camels and scorpions.

D

Memory game.

- Close your books. In groups, say sentences about one of the places.
- When you can't say a sentence (or your information is wrong) you are out!

Example: A: It is very hot in deserts.
 B: It is very dry.
 C: There are plants called cactuses.
 D: There are elephants.
 A: Wrong!

E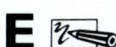

Write notes about where you live.

Place – Winnipeg, Canada
Climate – very cold and snowy in the winter/sunny in the summer
Plants – a lot of trees/flowers
Animals – bears/rabbits/birds

C

Read the text again and answer these questions.

1 In what continents are the tropical forests?
2 What fruits can you find in these forests?
3 How many kinds of insects can you find there?
4 How cold can it be in the Arctic?
5 Where can you find penguins?
6 How hot can it be in deserts?

Pronunciation

F

Listen to these words.

Group 1   *Group 2*
animal   plant

Listen and put the words in the correct group below.

Arctic / parrot / camel / Africa / banana / cactus / Antarctic / kangaroo / pineapple

Listen again and repeat the words.

Tsavo National Park, Kenya
A paradise for animal lovers.

Eiffel Tower, Paris
Come up and see Paris.

Hollywood, Los Angeles
Meet the stars.

The Amazon
The real forest.

Loch Ness, Scotland
Come and see the monster!

A

Look at the photos above. List three places you want to visit. Then think of two other places you want to visit.

Example: Kenya, Hollywood, Loch Ness, Disneyland and China

In groups, compare your lists. Then tell the class where your group wants to go.

Example: Three people want to go to Kenya.

B

Listen to two people talking about their travel plans. Which of the places in exercise A are they going to visit? Complete the first part of the table.

	Places to visit	Activities
Pamela		
Simon		

C 📼

Listen again and complete the second part of the table with these activities.

- learning a language
- swimming
- cycling
- camping

Language focus: GOING TO (PLANS)

D
Look at these examples.

> I'm **going to** learn.
> I'm **not going to** stay there all the time.
> You're **going to** go there!
> What are you **going to** do?
> We're **going to** visit my aunt.
> We **aren't going to** visit San Francisco.

Now copy and complete the tables below.

AFFIRMATIVE			
I	. . . . .		
You	. . . . .	going to	learn French.
He / She / (It)	is		
We / You / They	. . . . .		

NEGATIVE				
I	. . . . .			
You	. . . . .	not	going to	stay there.
He / She / (It)	is			
We / You / They	. . . . .			

QUESTION			
	am	I	
What	. . . . .	you	going to do?
	is	he / she / (it)	
	. . . . .	we / you / they	

E
Complete the sentences.

Example: 1 Pamela is going to stay with her family.

1 Pamela . . . . . stay with her family.
2 What are they . . . . . do?
3 . . . . . (you) learn Greek?
4 Simon . . . . . (not) visit Italy.
5 We . . . . . visit Athens.
6 They . . . . . (not) stay in London.

F
Write six sentences about where you are going to go and what you are going to do in the holidays.

I'm going to play tennis.

G

In pairs, find out what your partner is going to do in the holidays. You can only ask yes/no questions. The first person to find out three things is the winner!

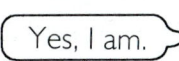

Are you going to swim in the sea?

Yes, I am.

A

Look at the pictures about Yind and Yanda's adventure. Put the paragraphs below in order. Then listen to the story and check your answers.

Example: 1 = D

A
Yind and Yanda escaped from the forest and came to the desert of Darga. They didn't have any water and it was very hot. Then hundreds of Dargans attacked them. The Dargans took Yind and Yanda to their village.

B
Suddenly a big spaceship arrived. The Dargans disappeared and a group of Zorgon tourists came out of the spaceship. The Zorgons were very friendly and they took Yind and Yanda back to the planet Alpha.

C
Their spaceship crashed on the planet Gondarg, in the horrible forests of Gondarg. There were enormous trees, snakes and giant scorpions.

D
A brother and a sister called Yind and Yanda lived on the planet Alpha. One day they decided to explore space in their parents' spaceship.

B

Listen again. True or false?

1 The planet Alpha was very beautiful.
2 Yind and Yanda went out with their parents.
3 After two hours Yind and Yanda crashed on Gondarg.
4 They walked for a long time.
5 One of the Dargans had a big knife.
6 Yind and Yanda invited the Dargans to a party.

3

4

C

Think of three questions to ask your group about their next holiday.

Example: What sport are you going to do?

Ask your questions and then write sentences about the information.

Example: Four people are going to go swimming.

D LEARN TO LEARN

In pairs, ask how your partner is going to learn English in the holidays. Are you going to:

– listen to songs in English?
– see English words?
– watch films in English?
– hear people talking English?
– speak English?
– read or write English?

Use these words to answer.

- Yes, definitely.
- Possibly.
- No, definitely not.

Project

E

Make a poster about a real or an imaginary country.

1 Choose a country and find out information about it, or invent the country and the information.

2 Write notes about these things.

- location (continent)
- area (square kilometres)
- population (millions)
- language(s)
- capital city and other cities
- climate (hot/cold)

3 Use your notes to write a description of the country.

4 Add these things to your poster.

- a map of the country
- a drawing of its flag
- photos or drawings of it

42 Language revision

Language practice

A

Write six sentences about what you are going to do this weekend.

Example: I'm going to play football. I'm going to do my English homework.

In pairs, suggest doing these things to your partner.

Example: A: What about playing football?
B: Okay, let's do that.
A: Why don't we do our homework?
B: No, thanks!

Vocabulary

B

Check you have all this information for the words in your vocabulary book.

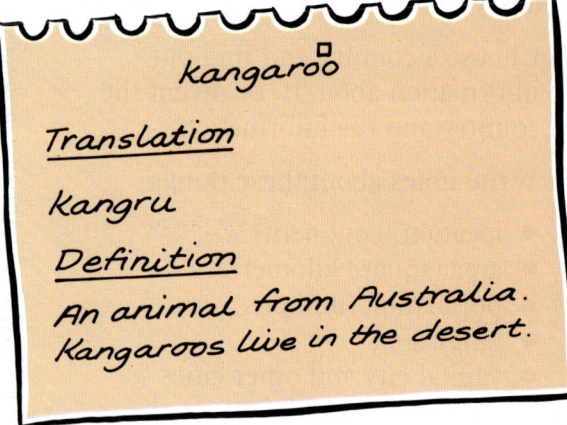

kangaroo

Translation

Kangru

Definition

An animal from Australia. Kangaroos live in the desert.

In pairs, test your partner about some of the words in your book.

Example: A: How do you spell *scorpion*?
B: S–C–O–R–P–I–O–N.
A: How do you say *león* in English?
B: Lion.

C

Find six words about clothes and seven about the climate.

T	R	O	U	S	E	R	S
R	R	A	I	N	Y	S	S
I	A	B	L	O	U	S	E
H	O	T	O	W	O	K	R
S	U	N	N	Y	C	I	D
T	A	O	C	R	I	R	A
D	C	O	L	D	H	T	T

Pronunciation

D

Listen to these words.

Group 1	*Group 2*
Morocco (short)	going (long)

Listen and put the words below into the correct group.

clothes / hot / cold / polar / fox / coat / snowy / hobby / holiday / ocean / okay /

Listen again and repeat the words.

Test yourself

E

Complete this dialogue.

A: Fantastic! The holidays are here!
B: What [1] . . . . . do?
A: Well, we [2] . . . . . visit my grandparents.
B: Lucky you! I [3] . . . . . stay here. This year we [4] . . . . . (not) go away.
A: What about this weekend? Why [5] . . . . . go to the cinema on Saturday afternoon?
B: No, thanks. I went yesterday. [6] . . . . . going to the swimming pool on Saturday?
A: Okay, let's do that.

F

Put the verbs in brackets in the present simple or present continuous.

Example: 1 = is eating

In the picture you can see four scorpions. One (eat) [1] . . . . . a small insect, another (sleep) [2] . . . . . under a rock and another (attack) [3] . . . . . a spider. The last scorpion is a female. She (carry) [4] . . . . . some baby scorpions.

Scorpions (live) [5] . . . . . in different places in the world, especially in hot places like deserts. They (not need) [6] . . . . . water for months.

Scorpions (have got) [7] . . . . . six legs and eight or ten eyes. Baby scorpions (stay) [8] . . . . . with their mother for a week. After that the little scorpions (leave) [9] . . . . . their mother. They are very aggressive and often they (attack) [10] . . . . . and (eat) [11] . . . . . their brothers and sisters!

G

Do the Module check on page 92.

Do the Module check on page 92.

Language check

PRESENT SIMPLE / PRESENT CONTINUOUS

Present simple
He **wears** strange clothes.
They **eat** rocks.

Present continuous
He **is wearing** a jacket now.
They **are eating** fruit and vegetables now.

SUGGESTIONS

Let's play chess.
Why don't we go to the park?
What about having lunch?

GOING TO (PLANS)

Affirmative
I'm **going to fly** to Toronto.
He / She / It's **going to visit** Hollywood.
You / We / They're **going to visit** San Francisco.

Negative
I'm **not going to fly** to Toronto.
He / She / (It) **isn't going to visit** Hollywood.
You / We / They **aren't going to visit** San Francisco.

Questions
Are you / we / they **going to fly** to Toronto?

Module check

Write the answers in your notebook.

General

1
What is your favourite lesson in this module?

Example: Holidays

2
Who is your favourite person?

Example: Eric the Red

3
What is your favourite picture?

Example: The Hindenburg pictures.

4
What is your favourite activity?

Example: The project

Speaking

5
Give yourself a mark for the speaking activities in this module.

5 – Very good: no problems.
4 – Good. No important problems.
3 – OK: some problems.
2 – Difficult.
1 – Impossible!

Reading and listening

6
Look at the reading (**R**) and listening (**L**) activities in the module. Put them in these groups.

Easy Aquapark (R)

OK Interviews: getting to school (L)

Difficult Gulliver's travels (L)

Grammar and vocabulary

7
Do the *Test yourself.* Write down your marks.

Example: 9/15

8
Look at the *Language check.* Give yourself a mark out of five for the structures (use the scale from number 5).

Example: Can = 4/5

9
Look at the *Useful vocabulary* section in the Activity Book. Check the words in your vocabulary book.

Irregular verb list

buy	bought
come	came
drink	drank
eat	ate
fight	fought
find	found
fly	flew
go	went
grow	grew
hide	hid
hold	held
learn	learned/learnt
leave	left
make	made
meet	met
put	put
read	read
ride	rode
run	ran
sell	sold
shoot	shot
sing	sang
sit	sat
sleep	slept
stand	stood
swim	swam
take	took
teach	taught
throw	threw
understand	understood
wear	wore
write	wrote

Phonetic chart

CONSONANTS

symbol	key word
/ p /	pen
/ b /	back
/ t /	tea
/ d /	day
/ k /	key
/ g /	get
/ tʃ /	cheer
/ dʒ /	jump
/ f /	fat
/ v /	view
/ θ /	thing
/ ð /	then
/ s /	soon
/ z /	zero
/ ʃ /	fish
/ ʒ /	pleasure
/ h /	hot
/ m /	come
/ n /	sun
/ ŋ /	sung
/ l /	led
/ r /	red
/ j /	yet
/ w /	wet

VOWEL

symbol	key word
/ i: /	sheep
/ ɪ /	ship
/ e /	bed
/ æ /	bad
/ ɑ: /	calm
/ ɒ /	pot
/ ɔ: /	saw
/ ʊ /	put
/ u: /	boot
/ ʌ /	cut
/ ɜ: /	bird
/ə/	China

DIPHTHONGS

symbol	key word
/ eɪ /	make
/ əʊ /	note
/ aɪ /	bite
/ aʊ /	now
/ ɔɪ /	boy
/ ɪə /	here
/ eə /	there
/ ʊə /	tour

Countries, continents and nationalities

1 Morocco / Moroccan
2 Europe / European
3 China / Chinese
4 Turkey / Turkish
5 Japan / Japanese
6 America / American
7 Portugal / Portuguese
8 Argentina / Argentinian
9 Italy / Italian
10 Brazil / Brazilian
11 Greece / Greek
12 Asia / Asian
13 South America / South American

Mini-dictionary

We recommend that you refer to **Longman New Junior English Dictionary** (first published 1984), for words not included here. Remember that this mini-dictionary is not a substitute for a complete dictionary.

accident /'æksɪdənt/ *noun* something (usually bad) that happens by chance: *Two cars had an* **accident**.

activity /æk'tɪvɪtɪ/ *noun* something you do: *Reading is my favourite* **activity**.

activity book /æk'tɪvɪtɪ bʊk/ *noun* see *Classroom objects*, page 103.

act /ækt/ *noun* something you do in front of an audience: *we saw a good circus* **act**.

actor /'æktə/ *noun* see *People*, page 104.

adult /'ædʌlt/ *noun* a person who is over eighteen years old.

adventure /əd'ventʃə/ *noun* an exciting story or journey. *adjective an* **adventure** *story; an* **adventure** *holiday*.

adventurous /əd'ventʃərəs/ *adjective* liking excitement or danger: *She likes climbing mountains – she's* **adventurous**.

advice /əd'vaɪs/ *noun* something to say to help somebody with a problem.

afternoon /'ɑːftə'nuːn/ *noun* the time between midday and about six o'clock.

age /eɪdʒ/ *noun* how old you are: *His* **age** *is twelve.* = *He's twelve years old.*

aggressive /ə'gresɪv/ *adjective* violent; not calm or quiet.

air hostess /'ɛə həʊstɪs/ *noun* see *People*, page 104.

airship /'ɛəʃɪp/ *noun*

alien /'eɪlɪən/ *noun* a creature from another planet.

alligator /'ælɪgeɪtə/ *noun* see *Animals*, page 102.

animal /'ænɪməl/ *noun* a living thing which is not a plant: *Fish, mammals and insects are* **animals**.

ant /ænt/ *noun* see *Animals*, page 102.

apple /'æpl/ *noun* see *Food and drink*, page 106.

arm /ɑːm/ *noun* see picture, Lesson 36, page 78.

arrive /ə'raɪv/ *verb* to get to a place: *They* **arrived** *at the hotel*.

arrow /'ærəʊ/ *noun* a weapon.

arrow

attack /ə'tæk/ *verb* to start to fight somebody: *The cowboys* **attacked** *the Indians*.

attic /'ætɪk/ *noun* a small room at the top of a house in the roof.

aunt /ɑːnt/ *noun* see *Families*, page 103.

B

baby /'beɪbɪ/ *noun* a very young child (or animal).

babysitter /'beɪbɪsɪtə/ *noun* a person who looks after the children when the parents are not at home.

back /bæk/ *noun* part of your body.

back

back door /bæk 'dɔː/ *noun* see *House*, page 105.

bad /bæd/ *adjective* not good.

badge /bædʒ/ *noun* see picture, Lesson 8, page 22.

badminton /'bædmɪntən/ *noun* a game like tennis.

badminton

bag /bæg/ *noun* see *Classroom objects*, page 103.

balloon /bə'luːn/ *noun* see picture, Lesson 9, page 25.

banana /bə'nɑːnə/ *noun* see *Food and drink*, page 106.

bank /bæŋk/ *noun* a building where you put and keep money.

bar /bɑː/ *noun* a place where you can buy and drink drinks.

barber /'bɑːbə/ *noun* see *People*, page 104.

basket /'bæskɪt/ *noun* a bag or container made out of straw.

basket

beach /biːtʃ/ *noun* the place next to the sea: *We play football on the* **beach**.

bear /bɛə/ *noun* see *Animals*, page 102.

beautiful /'bjuːtɪfʊl/ *adjective* good-looking; attractive.

bedroom /'bedrʊm/ *noun* see *House*, page 105.

bee /biː/ *noun* see *Animals*, page 102.

bicycle /'baɪsɪkl/ *noun*

big /bɪg/ *adjective* of great size, height or weight; large; not small.

bicycle

biography /baɪ'ɒgrəfɪ/ *noun* the story of somebody's life.

bird /bɜːd/ *noun* see *Animals*, page 102.

birthday /'bɜːθdeɪ/ *noun* the day you were born: *My* **birthday** *is on 15th September*.

block /blɒk/ *noun* see picture, Lesson 9, page 25.

blond /blɒnd/ *adjective* see picture, Lesson 5, page 16.

blood /blʌd/ *noun* the red liquid that goes round your body.

blouse /blaʊz/ *noun* see picture, Lesson 36, page 79.

board game /'bɔːd geɪm/ *noun* see picture, Lesson 9, page 24.

boat /bəʊt/ *noun*

bone /bəʊn/ *noun*

boat

bone

book /bʊk/ *noun* see *Classroom objects*, page 103.

boring /'bɔːrɪŋ/ *adjective* not interesting: *The film was* **boring** *and I fell asleep*.

born /bɔːn/ *adjective* given life: *She was* **born** *in 1991*.

bottle /'bɒtl/ *noun* see picture, Lesson 4, page 14.

bread /bred/ *noun* see picture, Lesson 33, page 72.

breakfast /'brekfəst/ *noun* the first meal you eat in the morning.

brilliant /'brɪljənt/ *adjective* very good: *I saw a* **brilliant** *film*.

brother /'brʌðə/ *noun* see *Families*, page 103.

buffalo /'bʌfələʊ/ *noun* see *Animals* page 102.

building /'bɪldɪŋ/ *noun* a place made of materials, e.g. a house, a cinema.

bus /bʌs/ *noun*

bus

bus driver /'bʌs draɪvə/ *noun* see *People* page 104.

businessman /'bɪznɪsmæn/ *noun* see *People*, page 104.

businesswoman /'bɪznɪswʊmən/ *noun* see *People*, page 104.

buy /baɪ/ *verb* to give money for something: *He **buys** a newspaper every day.*

C

cabin /'kæbɪn/ *noun* a small house made of wood.

cake /keɪk/ *noun* see picture, Lesson 16, page 38.

camel /'kæməl/ *noun* see *Animals*, page 102.

camera /'kæmrə/ *noun*

camping holiday /'kæmpɪŋ hɒlɪdeɪ/ *noun* a holiday where you live in a tent.

camera

can /kæn/ *noun* a metal container with food or drink in it: *A **can** of cola.*

canary /kə'nɛərɪ/ *noun* see *Animals*, page 102.

capital /'kæpɪtl/ *noun* the city where a country's government is: *Rome is the **capital** of Italy.*

car /kɑ:/ *noun*

car

cards /kɑ:dz/ *noun* see picture, Lesson 9, page 24.

carefully /'kɛəfəlɪ/ *adverb* with care and attention.

carrot /'kærət/ *noun* see *Food and drink*, page 106.

carry /'kærɪ/ *verb* to hold something and take it somewhere: *I **carry** my bag to school.*

cartoon /kɑ:'tu:n/ *noun* drawings which tell a story: *A Disney **cartoon**.*

cassette /kə'set/ *noun*

cassete

cat /kæt/ *noun* see *Animals*, page 102.

CD /si: di:/ *noun* compact disc.

ceiling /'si:lɪŋ/ *noun* see *House*, page 105.

change /tʃeɪndʒ/ *verb* to become or make different: *He **changed** the pictures in his room.*

channel /'tʃænl/ *noun* a television company, e.g. the BBC.

character /'kærɪktə/ *noun* a person in a book or film.

cheap /tʃi:p/ *adjective* costing little money: *I bought a **cheap** hat.*

cheese /tʃi:z/ *noun* see *Food and drink*, page 106.

chess /tʃes/ *noun* see picture, Lesson 8, page 22.

chicken /'tʃɪkɪn/ *noun* see *Food and drink*, page 106.

chief /tʃi:f/ *noun* the leader of a tribe of Indians.

child /tʃaɪld/ *(plural* **children***) /*'tʃɪldrən/) *noun* **1** a young person **2** a son or daughter.

church /tʃɜ:tʃ/ *noun*

church

cinema /'sɪnəmə/ *noun* a place where you pay to watch a film.

circus /'sɜ:kəs/ *noun* a show performed by a group of acrobats, clowns, animals, etc. usually in a big tent.

city /'sɪtɪ/ *noun* a large town, e.g. London, Paris, New York.

climate /'klaɪmɪt/ *noun* the typical weather in a country or region: *Our country has a hot **climate**.*

climb /klaɪm/ *verb* to go up: *We **climbed** a mountain.*

close /kləʊz/ *verb* to shut: ***Close** the door, please.*

clothes /kləʊðz/ *noun* what you wear, e.g. shirt, jeans, coat.

coat /kəʊt/ *noun* see picture, Lesson 36, page 79.

coin /kɔɪn/ *noun* see picture, Lesson 8, page 22.

cola /'kəʊlə/ *noun* see *Food and drink*, page 106.

cold /kəʊld/ *adjective* not hot: *Snow is very **cold**.*

collect /kə'lekt/ *verb* to keep lots of things: *He **collects** stamps.*

colour /'kʌlə/ *noun* see *Colours*, page 103.

come /kʌm/ *verb* to move to the person speaking: *Are you **coming** with me? She **comes** from Dublin.* (= she was born in Dublin)

comedy /'kɒmɪdɪ/ *noun* a funny play or TV programme.

comfortable /'kʌmftəbl/ *adjective* nice, pleasant: *I sat in a **comfortable** chair.*

comic /'kɒmɪk/ *noun* something you read with funny stories and pictures.

competition /kɒmpɪ'tɪʃən/ *noun* when two people or teams try to see who is best at a sport or game.

computer /kəm'pju:tə/ *noun* a machine that stores information.

computer game /kəm'pju:tə geɪm/ *noun* a game you play on a computer.

continent /'kɒntɪnənt/ *noun* a large area of land, e.g. Europe, Africa.

cook /kʊk/ *noun* see *People*, page 104. *verb* to prepare food.

cooker /'kʊkə/ *noun* see *House*, page 105.

country /'kʌntrɪ/ *noun* **1** a nation with a government, e.g, Portugal, Argentina **2** rural areas; not the city.

cover /'kʌvə/ *verb* to put something over another thing.

cow /kaʊ/ *noun* see *Animals*, page 102.

cowboy /'kaʊbɔɪ/ *noun* see *People*, page 104.

crash /kræʃ/ *verb* to move into another object with force: *The car **crashed** into the bus/tree/wall.*

crisps /krɪsps/ *noun* see *Food and drink*, page 106.

cross /krɒs/ *verb* to travel to the other side of something: *She **crossed** the room/road/river.*

cupboard /'kʌbəd/ *noun* see *House* page 105.

curious /'kjʊərɪəs/ *adjective* strange; unusual: *I heard a **curious** noise.*

cycle /'saɪkl/ *verb* to go by bicycle: *She **cycles** to school.*

D

dance /dɑ:ns/ *verb* to move to music: *We **danced** to the pop record.*

dangerous /'deɪndʒrəs/ *adjective* something that can hurt you: *Don't play with fire – it's **dangerous**.*

dark /dɑ:k/ *adjective* see picture, Lesson 5, page 16.

daughter /'dɔ:tə/ *noun* see *Families*, page 103.

decide /dɪ'saɪd/ *verb* to choose to do something: *We **decided** to have a party.*

definitely /'defɪnɪtlɪ/ *adverb* for sure; for certain.

dentist /'dentɪst/ *noun* see *People*, page 104.

desert /'dezət/ *noun* a very dry area with not many plants or animals.

desert island /dezət 'aɪlənd/ *noun* an island where nobody lives.

destination /destɪn'eɪʃən/ *noun* the place at the end of your journey.

dictionary /'dɪkʃənrɪ/ *noun* see *Classroom objects*, page 103.

die /daɪ/ *verb* to stop living: *He **died** in 1956.*

different /'dɪfrənt/ *adjective* not the same: *French and Spanish are **different** languages.*

difficult /'dɪfɪkəlt/ *adjective* not easy; hard: *This maths problem is **difficult**.*

dining room /'daɪnɪŋ rʊm/ *noun* see *House*, page 105.

dinosaur /'daɪnəsɔː/ *noun* see picture, Lesson 9, page 25.

disappear /dɪsə'pɪə/ *verb* to go away; be no longer seen: *The boy* **disappeared** *round the corner.*

disco /'dɪskəʊ/ (*noun* **discotheque**) a place where you dance to loud pop music.

doctor /'dɒktə/ *noun* see *People*, page 104.

doctor's surgery /dɒktəz 'sɜːdʒərɪ/ *noun* a place where a doctor sees patients.

dog /dɒg/ *noun* see *Animals*, page 102.

doll /dɒl/ *noun* see picture, Lesson 8, page 22.

dolphin /'dɒlfɪn/ *noun* see picture, Lesson 9, page 25.

dominoes /'dɒmɪnəʊz/ *noun* see picture, Lesson 9, page 24.

door /dɔː/ *noun* see *House*, page 105.

downstairs /daʊn'stɛəz/ *noun* see *House*, page 105.

dragon /'drægən/ *noun* see picture, Lesson 9, page 25.

dress /dres/ *noun* see picture, Lesson 36, page 79.

drink /drɪŋk/ *noun* see *Food and drink*, page 106. **drink** *verb* to take liquid in the mouth: *He* **drinks** *milk for breakfast.*

dry /draɪ/ *adjective* not wet; with no water.

duck /dʌk/ *noun* see *Animals*, page 102.

E

ear /ɪə/ *noun* see picture, Lesson 36, page 78.

easy /iːzɪ/ *adjective* not hard to do: *My homework was* **easy** *– I did it in five minutes.*

eat /iːt/ *verb* to take food in the mouth: *She* **eats** *a lot of fruit.*

egg /eg/ *noun* see *Food and drink*, page 106.

electricity /ɪlek'trɪsɪtɪ/ *noun* power for television, lights, fridges, etc.

elephant /'elɪfənt/ *noun* see picture, Lesson 2, page 11.

enormous /ɪ'nɔːməs/ *adjective* very big.

enter /entə/ *verb* to go in.

escape /ɪ'skeɪp/ *verb* to run away from a person or place: *He* **escaped** *from the police.*

evening /'iːvnɪŋ/ *noun* the time from the end of the afternoon to when you go to bed.

excellent /'eksələnt/ *adjective* very good.

exciting /ɪk'saɪtɪŋ/ *adjective* causing strong emotions: *I saw an* **exciting** *football match.*

expedition /ekspɪ'dɪʃən/ *noun* a journey with a specific purpose, usually scientific or military.

expensive /ɪks'pensɪv/ *adjective* costing a lot of money: *A Mercedes is an* **expensive** *car.*

explode /ɪks'pləʊd/ *verb* to burst with a loud noise: *The bomb* **exploded**.

explore /ɪks'plɔː/ *verb* to see and investigate a place for the first time.

eye /aɪ/ *noun* see picture, Lesson 5, page 16.

F

factory /'fæktərɪ/ *noun* a place where people work and make things: *a car* **factory**.

family /'fæmɪlɪ/ *noun* see *Families*, page 103.

famous /'feɪməs/ *adjective* well-known: *Prince is a* **famous** *singer.*

fantastic /fæn'tæstɪk/ *adjective* very good.

farm /fɑːm/ *noun* a place in the country where you grow food or keep animals.

farmer /fɑːmə/ *noun* a person who lives and works on a farm.

fat /fæt/ *adjective* see picture, Lesson 5, page 16.

father /fɑːðə/ *noun* see *Families*, page 103.

favourite /feɪvərɪt/ *adjective* what you like a lot: *Prince is my* **favourite** *singer.*

female /fi:meɪl/ *adjective* see *Animals*, page 102.

festival /'festɪvəl/ *noun* a time when people in a community meet and have fun. There is a **festival** *in my town each year.*

fight /faɪt/ *verb* to use your body or weapons against somebody in a violent way.

film /fɪlm/ *noun* what you watch at the cinema.

find /faɪnd/ (*past* **found**) *verb* to see or get something after you have looked for it.

finish /'fɪnɪʃ/ *verb* to end: *The lesson* **finishes** *at four o'clock.*

fire /faɪə/ *noun* see *House*, page 105.

fish /fɪʃ/ *noun* see *Animals*, page 102.

fizzy drink /fɪzi 'drɪŋk/ *noun* see *Food and drink*, page 106.

flag /flæg/ *noun*

flower /'flaʊə/ *noun*

flower   flag

fly /flaɪ/ *noun* see *Animals*, page 102.

fly /flaɪ/ *verb* **1** how a bird travels in the air **2** to travel in a plane, airship, etc.

food /fuːd/ *noun* things you eat. See *Food and drink*, page 106.

foot /fʊt/ *noun*

football /fʊtbɔːl/ *noun* a sport where two teams kick a ball in a goal.

foot

forest /fɒrɪst/ *noun* an area with lots of trees.

fork /fɔːk/ *noun* see picture, Lesson 4, page 14.

fox /fɒks/ see *Animals*, page 102.

friend /frend/ *noun* a person you know and like.

friendly /frendli/ *adjective* kind and helpful.

front door /frʌnt dɔː/ *noun* see *House*, page 105.

fruit /fruːt/ *noun* see *Food and drink*, page 106.

fun /fʌn/ *noun* amusement; a good time: *Parties are* **fun**.

funny /fʌni/ *adjective* amusing; something or someone that makes you laugh: *He told a* **funny** *story.*

G

game /geɪm/ *noun* something you play for fun: *Let's have a* **game** *of chess.*

garage /gærɑːʒ/ *noun* a small building where you put a car.

garden /gɑːdn/ *noun* a place with grass and flowers.

gas /gæs/ *noun* not solid or liquid: *Hydrogen and oxygen are* **gases**.

general store /'dʒenərəl stɔː/ *noun* a local shop which sells lots of different things.

giant /'dʒaɪənt/ *adjective* very big *noun* a big monster.

glass /glɑːs/ *plural* (**glasses**) *noun*

globetrotter /gləʊbtrɒtə/ *noun* a person who travels a lot.

glass

go /gəʊ/ (*past:* **went** /went/) *verb* to move or travel: *I* **go** *to school by bus.*

goldfish /gəʊldfɪʃ/ *noun* see *Animals*, page 102.

good-looking /gʊd-lʊkɪŋ/ *adjective* pretty, attractive.

gorilla /gə'rɪlə/ *noun* see *Animals*, page 102.

grandfather /grændfɑːðə/ *noun* see *Families*, page 103.

grandma /ˈgrændmɑ:/ *noun* short form of grandmother.

grandmother /ˈgrænmʌðə/ *noun* see *Families*, page 103.

grandpa /ˈgrænpɑ:/ *noun* short of form of grandfather.

grape /ɡreɪp/ *noun* see *Food and drink*, page 106.

great /ɡreɪt/ *adjective* very good: *The party was* **great**!

grow up /ɡrəʊʌp/ (**past**: *grew* /ɡru:/) *verb* to get older; to become an adult.

guide /ɡaɪd/ *noun* see *People*, page 104.

gun /ɡʌn/ *noun* a weapon

gun

H

hair /heə/ *noun* see picture, Lesson 5, page 16.

haircut /ˈheəkʌt/ *noun* the style of your hair: *You go to the barber's or hairdresser's for a* **haircut**.

hamburger /ˈhæmbɜ:ɡə/ *noun* see *Food and drink*, page 106.

hand /hænd/ *noun*

hand

hat /hæt/ *noun* something you wear on your head.

head /hed/ *noun* see picture, Lesson 36, page 78.

heated /ˈhi:təd/ *adjective* made warm or hot: *A* **heated** *room/swimming pool*.

help /help/ *verb* to do something for another person: *I* **helped** *my mother tidy the house.*

hen /hen/ *noun* see picture, Lesson 4, page 14.

hide /haɪd/ *verb* to put in a place other people don't know: *Where did you* **hide** *the money?*

hippo /ˈhɪpəʊ/ *noun* see *Animals*, page 102.

hobby /ˈhɒbi/ *noun* something interesting you do in your free time.

hockey /ˈhɒki/ *noun* a sport where two teams hit a ball with a stick.

hold /həʊld/ (**past**: *held* /held/) *verb* to have something in your hand: *I am* **holding** *a pencil.*

home /həʊm/ *noun* the place where you live or are from.

homework /ˈhəʊmwɜ:k/ *noun* extra school work you do at home.

honey /ˈhʌni/ *noun* food that bees make.

horrible /ˈhɒrəbəl/ *adjective* not good; not nice.

horse /hɔ:s/ *noun* see *Animals*, page 102.

hot /hɒt/ *adjective* not cold: *It's very* **hot** *in the Sahara desert.*

hot dog /hɒt dɒɡ/ *noun* see *Food and drink*, page 106.

hotel /həʊˈtel/ *noun* a place you pay to sleep in: *She stayed at the Ritz* **Hotel**.

house /haʊs/ *noun* see *House*, page 105.

human /ˈhju:mən/ *noun* a person from the planet Earth.

hungry /ˈhʌnɡri/ *adjective* how you feel when you want something to eat.

hunt /hʌnt/ *verb* to look for and kill animals.

husband /ˈhʌzbənd/ *noun* see *Families*, page 103.

hydrogen /ˈhaɪdrədʒən/ *noun* a type of gas.

I

ice cream /aɪs ˈkr:m/ *noun* see *Food and drink*, page 106.

icy /ˈaɪsi/ *adjective* very cold.

important /ɪmˈpɔ:tənt/ *adjective* of great interest or consequence: *An* **important** *match. An* **important** *exam.*

incredible /ɪnˈkredəbəl/ *adjective* something you can't believe.

Indian /ˈɪndiən/ *noun* one of the original people who lived in America.

indoor /ˈɪndɔ:/ *adjective* inside a building: *An* **indoor** *tennis match.*

insect /ˈɪnsekt/ *noun* see *Animals*, page 102.

interesting /ˈɪntrətɪŋ/ *adjective* something that gets your attention: *I like this book – it's* **interesting**.

invite /ɪnˈvaɪt/ *verb* to ask somebody to do something nice with you: *I* **invited** *him to my party.*

island /ˈaɪlənd/ *noun* a piece of land surrounded by water.

J

jacket /ˈdʒækət/ *noun* see picture, Lesson 36, page 79.

jaguar /ˈdʒæɡjuə/ *noun* see *Animals*, page 102.

jeans /dʒi:nz/ *noun* see picture, Lesson 36, page 79.

job /dʒɒb/ *noun* work you (usually) get money for: *What's her* **job**? *She's a doctor.*

joke /dʒəʊk/ *noun* a short, funny story.

journey /ˈdʒɜ:ni/ *noun* when you go from one place to another: *I'm going on a* **journey** *to America.*

juggle /ˈdʒʌɡəl/ *verb* see picture, Lesson 10, page 26.

K

kangaroo /ˌkæŋɡəˈru:/ *noun* see picture, Lesson 2, page 11.

kill /kɪl/ *verb* to make a person or animal die.

kind[1] /kaɪnd/ *noun* a sort; type; group: *What* **kind** *of car have you got?*

kind[2] *adjective* nice; helpful: *She loves animals – she is* **kind** *to animals.*

kiss /kɪs/ *verb* see picture, Lesson 38, page 82.

kitchen /ˈkɪtʃən/ *noun* see *House*, page 105.

knife /naɪf/ (*plural* **knives** /naɪvz/) *noun* see picture, Lesson 4, page 14.

L

lamp /læmp/ *noun* see *House*, page 105.

land /lænd/ *noun* the dry part of the earth, not covered by the sea.

language /ˈlæŋɡwɪdʒ/ *noun* the words you use when you speak, e.g. French, German, Spanish.

learn /lɜ:n/ *verb* to study and remember something: *I* **learn** *English at school.*

leave /li:v/ (*past*: **left** /left/) *verb* to go away from a place: *The train* **leaves** *in five minutes.*

leg /leg/ *noun* see picture, Lesson 36, page 78.

lemonade /ˌleməˈneɪd/ *noun* see *Food and drink*, page 106.

leopard /ˈlepəd/ *noun* see *Animals*, page 102.

lesson /ˈlesən/ *noun* the time in a school day when you learn things: *We have three English* **lessons** *a week.*

letter /ˈletə/ *noun* something you write to or receive from another person: *I got a* **letter** *from my penfriend today.*

like /laɪk/ *verb* to find pleasant; to enjoy: *I* **like** *ice cream.*

lion /ˈlaɪən/ *noun* see picture, Lesson 2, page 10.

live /lɪv/ *verb* to exist; to spend your life: *Kangaroos* **live** *in Australia. She* **lives** *in Brazil.*

local /ˈləʊkəl/ *adjective* a place near where you live: *a* **local** *cinema.*

log cabin /lɒg ˈkæbən/ *noun* a small house made of wood.

long /lɒŋ/ *adjective* see picture, Lesson 5, page 16.

look /lʊk/ *verb* to point your eyes towards a thing: **Look** *at the blackboard.*

look after *verb* to care for: *I looked* **after** *my baby brother.*

lounge /laʊndʒ/ *noun* a room you can relax in.

love /lʌv/ *verb* to like very much.

lunch /lʌntʃ/ *noun* a meal you eat in the middle of the day.

M

magic /ˈmædʒɪk/ *noun* clever or strange tricks somebody does to amuse other people.

make /meɪk/ (*past* **made** /met/) *verb* to produce or create: *He* **makes** *model cars.*

male /meɪl/ *adjective* see *Animals,* page 102.

marry /ˈmæri/ *verb* to become husband and wife.

match /mætʃ/ *noun* see picture, Lesson 4, page 14.

meat /miːt/ *noun* see *Food and drink,* page 106.

meet /miːt/ (*past* **met** /met/) *verb* **1** to see and talk to somebody for the first time: *I met John at a party.* **2** to see somebody at a fixed time or place: **Meet** *me outside the cinema.*

milk /mɪlk/ *noun* see *Food and drink,* page 106.

model /ˈmɒdl/ *noun* a small version of something: *a* **model** *car.*

money /ˈmʌni/ *noun* what you use to buy things, e.g. dollars, pounds, pesetas.

monkey /ˈmʌŋki/ *noun* see picture, Lesson 4, page 14.

monster /ˈmɒnstə/ *noun* a big, frightening animal, usually invented.

month /mʌnθ/ *noun* one of the twelve parts of the year: *January.*

morning /ˈmɔːnɪŋ/ *noun* the time from when you wake up to midday.

mosque /mɒsk/ *noun* a building where Muslims go to pray.

mosque

mother /ˈmʌðə/ *noun* see *Families,* page 103.

mount /maʊnt/ *noun* short form of mountain.

mountain /ˈmaʊntən/ *noun*
mountain

mouth /maʊθ/ *noun* see picture, Lesson 36, page 78.

music /ˈmjuːzɪk/ *noun* pleasant sounds made with instruments.

musician /mjuːˈzɪʃən/ *noun* a person who plays a musical instrument.

N

name /neɪm/ *noun* what you are called: *My* **name** *is Eric.*

nasty /ˈnɑːsti/ *adjective* not nice; bad.

nature /ˈneɪtʃə/ *noun* the world of plants and animals.

need /niːd/ *verb* to want; to find necessary: *I* **need** *some more money.*

new /njuː/ *adjective* not old: *I've got a* **new** *bicycle.*

nice /naɪs/ *adjective* good: *This apple is* **nice.**

niece /ˈniːs/ *noun* the daughter of one's brother or sister.

night /naɪt/ *noun* the time of day when you usually sleep.

nobody /ˈnəʊbədi/ *noun* not one person: **Nobody** *saw the film.*

nose /nəʊz/ *noun* see picture, Lesson 5, page 16.

notebook /ˈnəʊtbʊk/ *noun* see *Classroom objects,* page 103.

number /ˈnʌmbə/ *noun* see *Numbers,* page 104.

O

ocean /ˈəʊʃən/ *noun* a very large area of water. e.g. *the Atlantic.*

okay /əʊˈkeɪ/ *adjective* not bad: *I think pop music is* **okay.**

old /əʊld/ *adjective* **1** not new: *I live in an* **old** *house.* **2** not young: *My grandmother is very* **old.** **3** your age: *How* **old** *are you?*

olive /ˈɒlv/ *noun* see *Food and drink,* page 106.

olive oil /ˈɒlv ˈɔːl/ *noun* a liquid you cook with made from olives.

open /ˈəʊpən/ *verb* to make something open, not closed: **Open** *your book at page 22.*

orange /ˈɒrəndʒ/ *noun* **1** a fruit. See *Food and drink,* page 106. a colour. See *Colours,* page 103.

orange juice /ˈɒrəndʒ dʒuːs/ *noun* a drink made from oranges.

ox /ɒks/ (*plural* **oxen** /ˈɒksən/) *noun* see *Animals,* page 102.

P

packet /ˈpækət/ *noun* a small paper or plastic container: *I ate a* **packet** *of crisps.*

paint /peɪnt/ *verb* to put colour on something: *We* **painted** *the room blue.*

panther /ˈpænθə/ *noun* see picture, Lesson 2, page 10.

paper /ˈpeɪpə/ *noun* see *Classroom objects,* page 103.

paradise /ˈpærədaɪs/ *noun* a very beautiful place.

parents /ˈpeərənts/ *noun* mother and father.

park /pɑːk/ *noun* a large open space in a town with grass and trees and sometimes a play area for children.

parrot /ˈpærət/ *noun* see picture, Lesson 2, page 11.

party /ˈpɑːti/ *noun* a meeting of friends to have fun, dance, play games, etc.

passenger /ˈpæsəndʒə/ *noun* a person who travels on a bus, train, etc.

pen /pen/ *noun* see *Classroom objects,* page 103.

pencil /ˈpensəl/ *noun* see *Classroom objects,* page 000.

penfriend /ˈpenfrend/ *noun* a person from another country you write letters to.

penguin /ˈpeŋgwən/ *noun* see picture, Lesson 2, page 10.

perform /pəˈfɔːm/ *verb* to do something, usually in a theatre: *The actor/singer* **performed** *well.*

person /ˈpɜːsən/ (*plural* **people** /ˈpiːpəl/) *noun* a man, woman or child.

pet /pet/ *noun* an animal that lives in your house.

petrol /ˈpetrəl/ *noun* liquid used to power car engines.

photo /ˈfəʊtəʊ/ *noun* a picture you take with a camera.

piano /piˈænəʊ/ *noun*

pick up /pɪk ʌp/ *verb* to take something in your hand: **Pick up** *your book.*

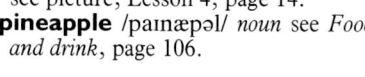
piano

pig /pɪg/ *noun* see picture, Lesson 4, page 14.

pineapple /ˈpaɪnæpəl/ *noun* see *Food and drink,* page 106.

piranha /pə'rɑːnjə/ *noun* see *Animals*, page 102.

place /pleɪs/ *noun* a situation: *We went to a nice* **place** *on our holiday.*

plane /pleɪn/ *noun* short form of aeroplane

plane

planet /plænət/ *noun* one of the large objects that move round the sun: *Jupiter, Mars, Saturn are* **planets**.

plant /plɑːnt/ *noun* see *House*, page 105.

plate /pleɪt/ *noun* see picture, Lesson 4, page 14.

play /pleɪ/ *verb* **1** to take part in a game: *I* **play** *football every day.* **2** to use a musical instrument: *I* **play** *the piano.*

pleasure park /pleʒə pɑːk/ *noun* a large outdoor area with entertainment: *Disneyworld is a* **pleasure park**.

polar bear /pəʊlə 'beə/ *noun* see *Animals*, page 102.

polar /pəʊlə/ *adjective* from the North or South Pole.

pole /pəʊl/ *noun* one of the points on the Earth of 90° latitude: *The North* **Pole** *is in the Arctic.*

policeman /pə'liːsmən/ **policewoman** /pə'liːswʊmən/ *noun* see *People*, page 104.

pool /puːl/ *noun* an area of water for swimming.

popular /pɒpjʊlə/ *adjective* when lots of people like something: *Super Quiz is a* **popular** *television programme.*

population /pɒpjʊleɪʃən/ *noun* the number of people in a place: *The* **population** *of Britain is 56 million.*

possibly /pɒsəbli/ *adverb* perhaps, maybe.

poster /pəʊstə/ *noun* see *House*, page 105.

potato /pə'teɪtəʊ/ *noun* see *Food and drink*, page 106.

pound /paʊnd/ *noun* a unit of British money: *Five* **pounds** *= £5.*

present /prezənt/ *noun* something somebody gives you: *My sister gave me a birthday* **present**.

president /prezədənt/ *noun* the head of a government.

problem /prɒbləm/ *noun* a difficult thing: *English spelling is a* **problem**.

programme /prəʊgræm/ *noun* something on television: *A children's* **programme**; *a sports* **programme**.

pull /pʊl/ *verb* to move something towards you: *He* **pulled** *a book out of his bag.*

put /pʊt/ (*past* **put**) *verb* to move something to a place: **Put** *the plates on the table.*

Q

quiz /kwɪz/ *noun* a competition where you test people by asking questions.

R

rabbit /ræbət/ *noun* see *Animals*, page 102.

radio /reɪdiəʊ/ *noun* see *House*, page 105.

railway station /reɪlweɪ steɪʃən/ *noun* a place where trains arrive and leave from.

rain /reɪn/ *noun* water that falls from the clouds.

rainy /reɪni/ *adjective* what the weather is like when it rains.

read /riːd/ (*past* **read** /red/) *verb* to look at and understand words: *I* **read** *a book yesterday.*

record /rekɔːd/ *noun* see picture, Lesson 8, page 22.

relax /rɪ'læks/ *verb* to rest from work.

restaurant /restərɒnt/ *noun* a place where you can buy and eat food.

return /rɪ'tɜːn/ *verb* to go back to a place.

rice /raɪs/ *noun* see *Food and drink*, page 106.

ride /raɪd/ (*past* **rode** /rəʊd/) *verb* to travel on a horse, bicycle or motorbike.

river /rɪvə/ *noun* a natural flow of water: *the* **river** *Nile.*

road /rəʊd/ *noun* what cars travel on; a street.

rock /rɒk/ *noun* a big stone.

rocking chair /rɒkɪŋ tʃeə/ *noun* see *House*, page 105.

rope /rəʊp/ *noun* see picture, Lesson 10, page 23.

rubber /rʌbə/ *noun* see *Classroom objects*, page 103.

rugby /rʌgbi/ *noun* a sport played with a ball like this:

rugby ball

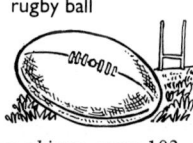

ruler /ruːlə/ *noun* see *Classroom objects*, page 103.

run /rʌn/ (*past* **ran** /ran/) *verb* to move very quickly on your feet: *I was late so I* **ran** *to school.*

S

sail /seɪl/ *verb* to travel by boat or ship.

saloon /sə'luːn/ *noun* see picture, Lesson 23, page 52.

salmon /sæmən/ *noun* see picture, Lesson 32, page 70.

sandwich /sænwidʒ/ *noun* see *Food and drink*, page 106.

scarf /skɑːf/ (*plural* **scarves** /skɑːvz/ *noun* something you wear round your neck. See picture, Lesson 12, page 32.

school /skuːl/ *noun* a place where you study.

scorpion /skɔːpiən/ *noun* see *Animals*, page 102.

seaside /siːsaɪd/ *noun* a holiday place near the sea.

sell /sel/ (*past* **sold** /səʊld/) *verb* to change something for money: *They* **sell** *sweets in the shop.*

shake /ʃeɪk/ (*past* **shook** /ʃʊk/) *verb* to move quickly from side to side or up and down: *I said hello and* **shook** *his hand.*

shark /ʃɑːk/ *noun* see *Animals*, page 102.

sheep /ʃiːp/ (*plural* **sheep**) *noun* see *Animals*, page 102.

sheriff /ʃerəf/ *noun* see *People*, page 104.

ship /ʃɪp/ *noun*

shirt /ʃɜːt/ *noun* see picture, Lesson 36, page 79.

ship

shoe /ʃuː/ *noun* see picture, Lesson 36, page 79.

shoot /ʃuːt/ (*past* **shot** /ʃɒt/) *verb* to use a gun.

shop /ʃɒp/ *noun* a place where you can buy things: *a toy* **shop**; *a clothes* **shop**.

short /ʃɔːt/ *adjective* see picture, Lesson 5, page 16.

shout /ʃaʊt/ *verb* to speak very, very loudly.

show /ʃəʊ/ *verb* to let someone see something: *I* **showed** *him my toys.*

silly /sɪli/ *adjective* not serious or sensible.

sing /sɪŋ/ (*past* **sang** /sɑːŋ/) *verb* to make music with your voice.

singer /sɪŋə/ *noun* see *People*, page 104.

sister /sɪstə/ *noun* see *Families*, page 103.

sit /sɪt/ (*past* **sat** /sæt/) *verb* to rest on the bottom of your back: *He* **sat** *on a chair.*

skin /skɪn/ *noun* the outside of your body or an animal's body: *An elephant's* **skin** *is hard and grey.*

skirt /skɜ:t/ *noun* see picture, Lesson 36, page 79.

skis /ski:z/ *noun*

skis

sleep /sli:p/ (*past* **slept** /slept/) *verb* to rest with your eyes closed: *I usually* **sleep** *for seven hours a night.*

slow /sləʊ/ *adjective* not fast; at a low speed. *He is a* **slow** *worker.*

slowly /sləʊli/ *adverb* to do something in a slow manner: *He walks very* **slowly.**

small /smɔ:l/ *adjective* not big. See picture, Lesson 5, page 16.

smell /smel/ *noun* something you detect with your nose: *There's a strong* **smell** *of coffee in this room.*

smile /smaɪl/ *verb* move your mouth to show you are happy.

smile

snake /sneɪk/ *noun* see *Animals*, page 102.

snow /snəʊ/ *noun* very cold rain which is soft and white.

snowy /snəʊi/ *adjective* what the weather is like when it snows.

sofa /səʊfə/ *noun* see *House*, page 105.

somebody /sʌmbɒdi/ *noun* any person: *If you don't know the answer, ask* **somebody.**

somersault /sʌməsɔ:lt/ *noun* see picture, Lesson 10, page 26.

son /sʌn/ *noun* see *Families*, page 103.

spaceship /speɪsʃɪp/ *noun* a means of transport for travelling away from the Earth: *They went to the moon in a* **spaceship.**

spectacular /spek'tækjʊlə/ *adjective* wonderful; incredible; fantastic.

spider /spaɪdə/ *noun* see *Animals*, page 102.

sport /spɔ:t/ *noun* games in general: *Football and tennis are sports.*

sports car /spɔ:tskɑ:/ *noun* a fast car for two people.

spot /spɒt/ *noun* a small area: *This is a nice* **spot** *for a picnic.*

square /skweə/ *noun* an open area in the centre of a town or village.

stable /steɪbəl/ *noun* a place where you can put your horse or buy one.

stamp /stæmp/ *noun* see picture, Lesson 8, page 00.

stand /stænd/ (*past* **stood** /stʊd/) *verb* to be on your feet.

star /stɑ:/ *noun* a very famous person: *Prince is a* **star.**

start /stɑ:t/ *verb* to begin: *We* **start** *lessons at nine o'clock.*

station /steɪʃən/ *noun* a place where buses and trains arrive or leave from.

statue /stætʃu:/ *noun* a figure of a person (usually stone).

stay /steɪ/ *verb* to continue to be: *He* **stayed** *in the hotel for a week.*

stilts /stɪlts/ *noun* see picture, Lesson 10, page 26.

storm /stɔ:m/ *noun* very bad weather.

strange /streɪndʒ/ *adjective* unusual; not what you are accustomed to.

street /stri:t/ *noun* a road with buildings at the side of it.

strong /strɒŋ/ *adjective*: *This man is* **strong.**

student's book /stju:dənts bʊk/ *noun* see *Classroom objects*, page 103.

study /stʌdi/ *verb* to try to learn something: *I* **study** *English.*

subtitles /sʌbtaɪtls/ *noun* text in your language shown at the bottom of the picture during a foreign film.

sugar /ʃʊgə/ *noun* see *Food and drink*, page 106.

summer /sʌmə/ *noun* the part of the year from spring to autumn: *The weather is usually warm or hot in* **summer.**

sunny /sʌni/ *adjective* what the weather is like when it's hot and there are no clouds.

supermarket /su:pəmɑ:kət/ *noun* a large shop where you can buy lots of different types of food and drink and things for the house.

surface /sɜ:fəs/ *noun* the outside part or top of something: *The* **surface** *of a planet; the* **surface** *of a table.*

sweets /swi:ts/ *noun* see picture, Lesson 16, page 38.

swim /swɪm/ (*past* **swam** /swæm/) *verb* to move in water.

swimmer /swɪmə/ *noun* a person who swims

swimming pool /swɪmɪŋ pu:l/ *noun* a special place where you pay and go to swim.

swimmer

T

table /teɪbəl/ *noun* see *House*, page 105.

table tennis /teɪbəl tenəs/ *noun* a game for two people played with a ball and two bats on a table with a net.

take away /teɪk ə'weɪ/ (*past* **took** /tʊk/) *verb* to move from one place to another: **Take away** *these plates, please.*

take out /teɪk 'aʊt/ *verb* to remove from a container: *He* **took** *his book out of the bag.*

talk /tɔ:k/ *verb* to speak: *I* **talk** *to my friends.*

tall /tɔ:l/ *adjective* see picture, Lesson 5, page 16.

tarantula /tə'ræntjʊlə/ *noun* a very large spider.

taxi /tæksi/ *noun* a car which takes you on a journey which you pay for.

teach /ti:tʃ/ (*past* **taught** /tɔ:t/) *verb* to help a person to learn.

teacher /ti:tʃə/ *noun* see *People*, page 104.

team /ti:m/ *noun* a group of two or more people who play a game.

telephone /teləfəʊn/ *noun*

television /telɪvɪʒən/ *noun* see *House*, page 105.

telephone

temperature /tempərətʃə/ *noun* how hot or cold it is.

tennis /tenəs/ *noun* a sport where two (or four) people hit a ball over a net.

tent /tent/ *noun*

terrible /terəbəl/ *adjective* very bad.

tent

thin /θɪn/ *adjective* see picture, Lesson 5, page 16.

thousand /θaʊzənd/ *noun* a number = 1,000.

throw /θrəʊ/ (*past* **threw** /θru:/) *verb* to send something through the air with your arms.

tiger /taɪgə/ *noun* see picture, Lesson 2, page 10.

tightrope /taɪtrəʊp/ *noun* see picture, Lesson 10, page 26.

tipi /ti:pi:/ *noun* an American Indian tent.

tipi

toilet /tɔɪlət/ *noun* see *House*, page 105.

tomato /tə'mɑ:təʊ/ *noun* see *Food and drink*, page 106.

tourist /tʊərəst/ *noun* see *People*, page 104.

touring holiday /tʊərɪŋ hɒlədi/ *noun* see picture, Lesson 30, page 66.

town /taʊn/ *noun* a large group of buildings where people live and work.

toy /tɔɪ/ *noun* something a child plays with.

tractor /træktə/ *noun*

tractor

train /treɪn/ *noun*

transport /træn'spɔːt/ *noun* a way to travel: *Buses, cars and trains are forms of* **transport**.

travel /'trævəl/ *verb* to go from one place to another.

tree /triː/ *noun*

tropical /'trɒpɪkəl/ *adjective* from the tropics (hot areas of the world)

trousers /'traʊzəz/ *noun* see picture, Lesson 36, page 00.

t-shirt /'tiːʃɜːt/ *noun* see picture, Lesson 36, page 79.

turn on /tɜːn ɒn/ *verb* to start a machine: **Turn on** *the radio*.

TV /tiːviː/ *noun* short form of television.

U

understand /ʌndə'stænd/ (*past* **understood** /ʌndə'stʊd/) *verb* to hear or read something and know what it means.

unicycle /'juːnəsaɪkəl/ *noun* see picture, Lesson 10, page 26.

upstairs /ʌp'steəz/ *noun* see *House*, page 105.

use /juːz/ *verb* you employ a thing to do something else: *She* **used** *her new pen to write a story*.

useful /'juːsfəl/ *ajective* of use; helpful.

V

vegetable /'vedʒtəbəl/ *noun* see *Food and drink*, page 106.

video /'vɪdiəʊ/ *noun* a cassette to record films and television programmes.

village /'vɪlɪdʒ/ *noun* a small town; a group of houses.

villager /'vɪlɪdʒə/ *noun* a person who lives in a village.

vines /vaɪnz/ *noun* see picture, Lesson 32, page 70.

violent /'vaɪələnt/ *adjective* aggressive.

visit /'vɪzət/ *verb* to go and see a person or place: *He* **visits** *museums when he's on holiday*.

visitor /'vɪzət/ *noun* a person who visits a place.

W

waiter /'weɪtə/ *noun* see *People*, page 104.

waitress /'weɪtrəs/ *noun* a female waiter.

walk /wɔːk/ *verb* to move on your feet: *I* **walk** *to school every day*.

want /wɒnt/ *verb* to wish for something: *I'm hungry – I* **want** *a sandwich*.

warm /wɔːm/ *adjective* a temperature between cold and hot.

watch /wɒtʃ/ *verb* to look at (usually with interest).

water /'wɔːtə/ *noun* see *Food and drink*, page 106.

weapon /'wepən/ *noun* something you fight with: *Guns and arrows are* **weapons**.

wear /weə/ (*past* **wore** /wɔːə/) *verb* to have clothes on.

week /wiːk/ *noun* the seven days from Monday to Sunday.

weekend /wiːk'end/ *noun* the time from Friday evening to Sunday evening.

western /'westən/ *noun* a film about life in the Wild West.

wife /waɪf/ *noun* see *Families*, page 103.

wild /waɪld/ *adjective* not friendly or domesticated: *Lions are* **wild** *cats*.

window /'wɪndəʊ/ *noun* see *House*, page 105.

winter /'wɪntə/ *noun* the part of the year from autumn to spring: *The weather is usually cold in* **winter**.

wolf /wʊlf/ (*plural* **wolves** /'wʊlvz/) *noun* see *Animals*, page 102.

work /wɜːk/ *verb* to do your job: *He* **works** *in an office*.

world /wɜːld/ *noun* everything on our planet: *There are many countries in the* **world**.

worry /'wʌri/ *verb* to be concerned or nervous about something: *Don't* **worry** *about your exams*.

write /raɪt/ (*past* **wrote** /rɔːt/) *verb* to communicate using a pen and paper.

Y

young /jʌŋ/ *adjective* not old; of not many years: *She is three years old – she's very* **young**.

Picture dictionary

Animals

alligator

bear

rabbit

gorilla

hippo

camel

polar bear

snake

wolf

fox

buffalo

ox

horse

dog

spider

cow

female lion

jaguar

male lion

cat

scorpion

leopard

sheep

INSECTS

ant

fly

bee

canary

BIRDS

duck

FISH

goldfish

shark

piranha

Classroom objects

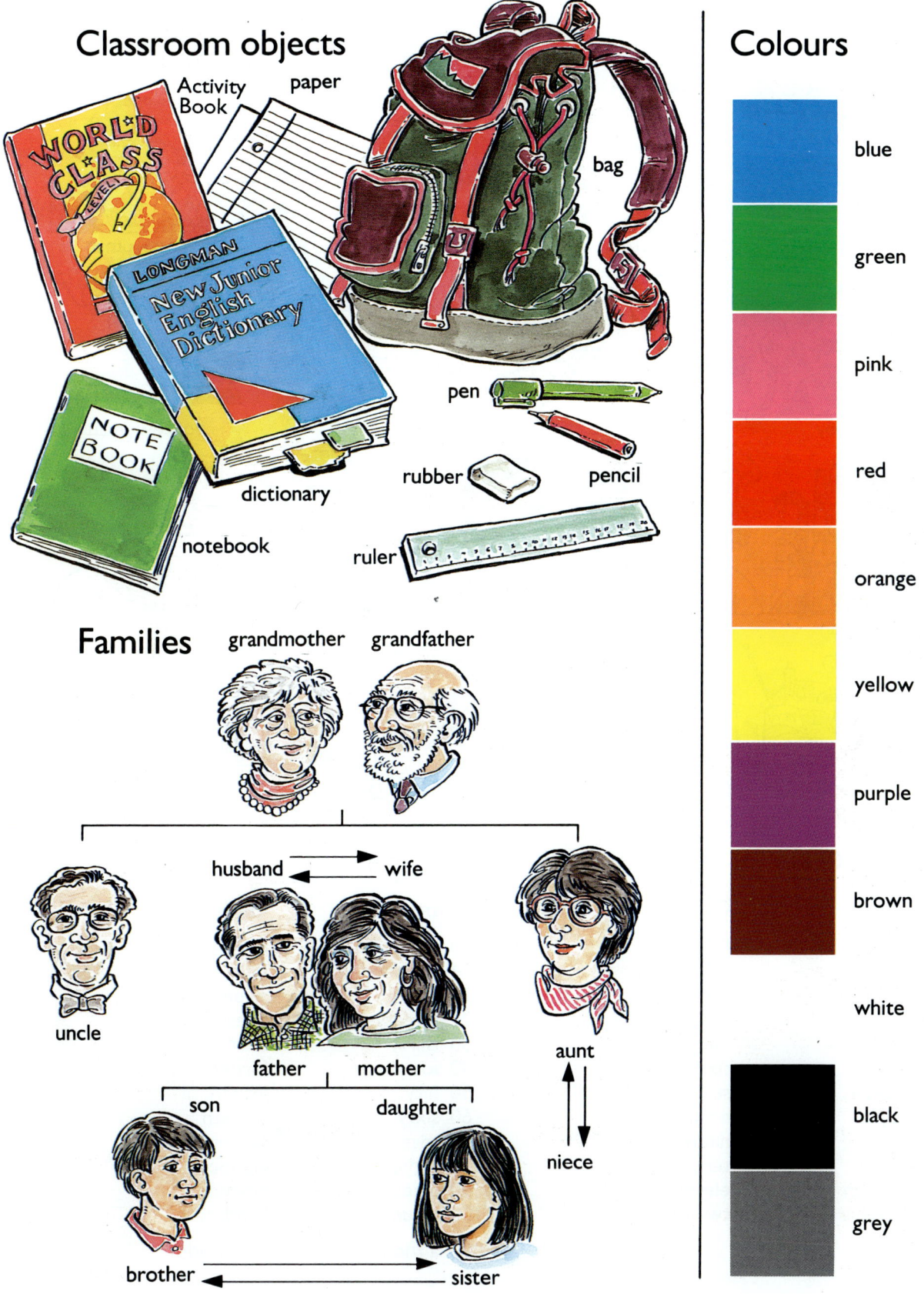

Activity Book

paper

WORLD CLASS

LONGMAN New Junior English Dictionary

NOTE BOOK

dictionary

notebook

bag

pen

rubber

pencil

ruler

Families

grandmother   grandfather

husband → ← wife

uncle

father   mother

aunt

niece

son   daughter

brother → ← sister

Colours

blue

green

pink

red

orange

yellow

purple

brown

white

black

grey

103

People

actor	air hostess	bus driver	businesswoman
cowboy	dentist	guide	policewoman
businessman	cook	tourist	barber	doctor
policeman	sheriff	teacher	waiter	vampire

Numbers

Number		Order	Number		Order
1	one	first	13	thirteen	thirteenth
2	two	second	14	fourteen	fourteenth
3	three	third	20	twenty	twentieth
4	four	fourth	21	twenty-one	twenty-first
5	five	fifth	30	thirty	thirtieth
6	six	sixth	40	forty	fortieth
7	seven	seventh	50	fifty	fiftieth
8	eight	eighth	60	sixty	sixtieth
9	nine	ninth	70	seventy	seventieth
10	ten	tenth	80	eighty	eightieth
11	eleven	eleventh	90	ninety	ninetieth
12	twelve	twelfth	100	a hundred	hundredth
			1000	a thousand	thousandth

House

bathroom
plant
ceiling
door
poster
bedroom
window
radio
toilet
upstairs

back door
kitchen
cupboard
cooker
fire
sofa
television
rocking chair
table
lamp
front door
dining room

downstairs

Food and drink

pineapple

hamburger

apple

orange

chicken

banana

grape

olive

cheese

hot dog

lemonade

water

cola

tomato

carrot

potato

milk

crisps

CRISPS
CHEESE AND ONION

fizzy drink

sandwich

rice

sugar

egg

ice cream